GOVERNING
BY NETWORK

GOVERNING BY NETWORK

The New Shape of the Public Sector

Stephen Goldsmith

William D. Eggers

INNOVATIONS IN AMERICAN GOVERNMENT
John F. Kennedy School of Government
Harvard University

BROOKINGS INSTITUTION PRESS
Washington, D.C.

Copyright © 2004
THE BROOKINGS INSTITUTION
1775 Massachusetts Avenue, N.W.
Washington, D.C. 20036
www.brookings.edu

Library of Congress Cataloging-in-Publication data

Goldsmith, Stephen, 1946–
Governing by network : the new shape of the public sector/Stephen Goldsmith, William D. Eggers.
    p.   cm.
Includes bibliographical references and index.
ISBN 0-8157-3128-0 (cloth : alk. paper)—
ISBN 0-8157-3129-9 (pbk : alk. paper)
    1. Public-private sector cooperation—United States. 2. Public administration—United States. 3. Contracting out—United States. I. Eggers, William D. II. Title.
JK421.G59 2004
352.3'7—dc22   2004019411

9 8 7 6 5 4 3 2 1

The paper used in this publication meets minimum requirements of the American National Standard for Information Sciences—Permanence of Paper for Printed Library Materials: ANSI Z39.48-1992.

Typeset in Sabon

Composition by Circle Graphics
Columbia, Maryland

Printed by R. R. Donnelley
Harrisburg, Virginia

Contents

Foreword

The job of running American government now faces a profound problem: much of what is written doesn't match much of the way government actually works. Consider the tragic disintegration of the space shuttle *Columbia* in February 2003. As it reentered the atmosphere over the southwestern United States, repeated efforts by ground control to raise the ship got no response. Horrified observers watched it break apart into thousands of pieces, and soon television viewers around the world saw, again and again, the sad end of the shuttle and its crew.

As investigators tried to piece together the clues, they discovered that a piece of foam insulation had broken off during launch and struck the edge of *Columbia*'s wing. NASA's cameras had detected the strike, but engineers concluded it was unlikely that it had caused serious damage. They were wrong. The small, light piece of foam had punched a hole in the shuttle's wing, and as the craft descended, hot gases flooded into the hole and caused the shuttle to break apart.

Why hadn't NASA officials detected the problem, warned the crew, and attempted some kind of emergency repair? Investigators concluded two things. First, NASA had no capability for such an in-flight repair. Second and more disturbing, NASA itself did not have the capacity for assessing the situation. As part of the agency's "faster, better, cheaper" strategy of the 1990s, virtually all of the operations—designing, building, launching, maintaining, and landing—to do with the shuttle had been turned over to a mega-contractor. The company, United Space Alliance (USA) was a hybrid contractor formed from Boeing and Lockheed Martin, the companies on which NASA had long relied for its manned space missions. United Space Alliance and its vast network of subcontractors did almost all the work on the shuttle and spent 90 percent of the shuttle's budget. NASA knew only the information that USA shared. It had no capacity for independent judgment, and it could not know what it did not think to ask. When the company's engineers concluded that the shuttle had been in no danger from the collision with the piece of foam, NASA had little choice but to accept the judgment. It did not have sufficient expertise of its own to do anything else. So, not only did NASA depend on its contractors to operate the shuttle, it had to rely on them for critical judgments about the safety of the system.

The accident would have been sad enough under any circumstances. But its grim echo of the circumstances that led to the 1986 explosion of the *Challenger* compounded the tragedy. The *Challenger* exploded because the rubber gaskets in its solid rocket motors failed. More than that, though, the *Challenger* accident resulted from NASA's inability to know what its contractors knew. NASA promised to fix the problems in its contract management and organizational culture, but the 2003 tragedy showed that the effort had fallen short. As the widower of one of *Columbia*'s astronauts sadly concluded, "I think we are really going to have to look very carefully at what lessons we didn't learn from *Challenger* and make sure we absolutely learn them this time."[1]

The inescapable conclusion is that without a deep change in NASA, such accidents are likely to recur. But one should not conclude that NASA is a tragically flawed government agency, constantly prone to catastrophe. Rather, it is a prime exhibit in the case that Stephen Goldsmith and William D. Eggers make in *Governing by Network*: government has come to rely far more on a vast complex of nongovernmental partners, but it has not yet figured out how to manage them well. There are huge advantages to the government's reliance on these networks of private contractors, state and local government grantees, and electronic partners. They give the government far more flexibility and the ability to tailor the service delivery system to better satisfy the demands of choice-driven citizens. Moreover, even if we wanted to retreat from government's growing reliance on these systems, they have become so deeply entrenched—politically and administratively—that there is no going back.

But if government has become ever more reliant on its network-based partnerships, we certainly have not figured out how best to make them work: how to make them administratively effective and how to hold them politically accountable. The central lesson of this lively, engaging, and important book is that we need to confront the realities of the system we have created and learn how to manage it well. *Governing by Network* is chock full of rich descriptions and lessons for how to deal with the emergence of governance by network. That makes it an invaluable guide to a government whose realities have outrun the leading theories.

The biggest insight that Goldsmith and Eggers bring to the debate is the need to reconcile traditional top-down hierarchy, built along vertical lines of authority, with emerging networks, built along horizontal lines of action. Traditional public administration starts with the organization as the basic building block, and it views the organization as a system in which top officials direct workers to accomplish its mission. More recently, formal approaches of bureaucracy have sought to understand the incentives of administrators and to use this analysis to construct a rigorous top-down model of bureaucratic behavior. But what happens when the job of accomplishing the mission lies outside the organization, when much of the work occurs through complex links among multiple organizations (public and private) that must be coordinated, and where most of the work of most government employees does not directly connect to those who accomplish the organization's mission? In a surprisingly large and growing part of government's action, these are precisely the patterns that shape results.

Goldsmith and Eggers are not shy about arguing that this is a good thing. They explore the dimensions of the movement in an uncommonly thorough and careful way. They chart how it departs from the traditional thinking about government and its operations, and they carefully explore its implications. And where practice departs from theory, as is often the case, they have built a foundation for helping to strengthen government's performance and its accountability.

As a result, this book is a singularly important contribution to thinking about governance in the twenty-first century. As this country's rich tradition of space flight demonstrates, government needs partners to do its work well. As the *Challenger* accident showed, networked government is a huge force that can have enormous implications. And as the *Columbia* accident demonstrated seventeen years later, if we do not learn the lessons of how to strengthen our ability to govern networks more effectively, we might well be doomed to repeat the tragedies of ineffective governance and fail to reap the considerable benefits that can—and should—flow from *governing by network*.

Donald F. Kettl
University of Pennsylvania

The Rise of
Governing by Network

ONE

The New Shape
of Government

On a crisp San Francisco morning in 1993, National Park Service superintendent Brian O'Neill got some good news and some bad news. The good news? The 76,000-acre Golden Gate National Recreational Area (GGNRA) that he oversaw had been given hundreds of acres of prime waterfront real estate just steps away from the Golden Gate Bridge. The bad news? The land, Crissy Field, was an environmental nightmare. For decades the Presidio military base had used it as an industrial storage yard, and by the time the military deeded it to the National Park Service, Crissy Field was loaded with upward of 87,000 tons of environmental contaminants. It would cost tens of millions of dollars to reclaim and improve the land, and Congress—naturally—had not allocated any money for the improvements.

The traditional response from a federal employee in O'Neill's situation would be to ask Congress for more money. Brian O'Neill, however, is not the typical federal manager. Instead, he paid a visit to his old friend Greg Moore, executive director of GGNRA's nonprofit partner, the Golden Gate Conservancy. "Let's try to raise the needed funds ourselves," proposed O'Neill. After a little persuading, Moore agreed to give it a try.

O'Neill's National Park Service colleagues were not so enthusiastic. Some thought his idea was crazy; after all, no one *voluntarily* gives money to the federal government. Others worried that if GGNRA succeeded in raising the funds, Congress would be less willing in the future to open its checkbook to park service projects.

O'Neill, characteristically, ignored the naysayers and with Moore's help plunged wholeheartedly into the enterprise. The result exceeded everyone's expectations—even O'Neill's. Not only did they raise more than $34 million for the renovation, but they also mustered unprecedented community support for the park. O'Neill even managed to convince dozens of nonprofit organizations to provide educational and environmental programs at Crissy Field. The end result: the concrete-laden environmental wasteland was transformed into a picturesque shoreline national park and environmental learning center.

By typical park service standards, this result would have been considered an extraordinary achievement. For Brian O'Neill and the staff at GGNRA, however, it was just another day at the office. During O'Neill's tenure, he and his team have partnered with hundreds of outside organizations. In fact, nonprofits do everything at the recreation area from maintaining historic buildings to rehabilitating stranded marine mammals. But outside involvement in the park extends beyond nonprofit contribution. Concessionaire firms provide tours of Alcatraz Island, contractors operate the park's housing rental program, and a real estate firm runs an international center for scientific, research, and educational activities. The partnerships are so extensive that National Park Service employees constitute only 18 percent of the GGNRA workforce; partners, concessionaires, contractors, cooperative associations, and volunteers compose the other 82 percent. "This park wants to partner," explains Alex Swisler, executive director of the Fort Mason Foundation, a nonprofit supporter of the park. "They talk about it and have made it part of the culture."

As a result of O'Neill's efforts, the Golden Gate National Recreational Area—which encompasses such breathtaking scenery as Stinson Beach, Muir Woods, Marin Headlands, Fort Point, and the Presidio—has become less like a government-run park and more like a network of interlocked public-private partnerships. Golden Gate operates on the premise that park employees should not do anything that the greater community could do as well or better.[1] O'Neill and his management team live up to this principle by establishing a vision, writing a strategic plan, and then seeking help from the broader community to make it a reality. "Within the broader community are people with a whole set of talents who can make things happen," explains O'Neill. "My job is to figure out who our strategic partners should be and how to bring them together and inspire them to be a part of it."

This partner-centric approach represents a radical departure from the way that most national parks operate. Since its inception in 1916, the National Park Service has had a reputation for cultivating an insular culture. "The philosophy has always been that the best way to do things was to do it yourself," explains O'Neill. "It was a fortress mentality—put a gate around the park and keep the community from interfering."

O'Neill felt that he had no choice but to work outside this model. An insular attitude simply would not work at Golden Gate; O'Neill and his colleagues maintain more than 1,000 historic buildings, steward 76,000 acres of environmentally sensitive land, and produce a steady diet of educational and environmental programming. GGNRA infrastructure needs run into the hundreds of millions of dollars. Relying solely on federal funding would have been a recipe for failure. "The only thing static or losing ground [in this situation] was our own budget," recalls O'Neill. Two of the park's most important partners, the Golden Gate Conservancy and the Fort Mason Foundation, contribute close to 20 percent of the park's total support each year. For the nearly twenty years of its existence, the conservancy has invested a whopping $70 million into the park. The Fort Mason Foundation has pitched in more than $18 million in physical improvements and oversees more than 40 nonprofit tenants and 15,000 program events annually on behalf of GGNRA. In its role as intermediary between the park service and the dozens of organizations that occupy space and deliver programs at Fort Mason, the foundation provides invaluable management assistance to O'Neill and his staff. "We can serve as a buffer between the park service and the nonprofits," says Fort Mason's Swisler. "This gives them [the nonprofits] greater flexibility and freedom than they might have if they were dealing directly with the federal government."

Another twenty or so nonprofits, together with one for-profit entity, operate and maintain GGNRA buildings and facilities on behalf of the park service. Under long-term lease arrangements, these organizations provide all the upkeep and capital improvements themselves. In fact, the Golden Gate National Recreational Area Park was the first national park to invite external service groups to occupy park buildings on its behalf. In all, partner organizations have contributed more than $100 million in capital improvements to the park since GGNRA was founded in 1972.

Such success has silenced the critics who dogged O'Neill and his team as they built this new management model. O'Neill has faced—and overcome—resistance from diverse camps, including environmentalists, who worried that some capital improvements would degrade the environment, and government lawyers, who sometimes were more skilled at hindering innovation than facilitating it. "When you're out there trying to do innovative stuff, there are a whole lot of people trying to bring you down," says O'Neill. "All sorts of folks hoped we'd fail."

Managing a governmental entity that achieves most of its mission through networks of partners requires an approach and skill set different from traditional government models. For example, how many executive leaders could conceptualize such a broad redefinition of their responsibilities and then implement the changes as O'Neill did? The average National Park Service employee tends to have professional and technical knowledge but lacks experience negotiating and collaborating with outside organizations—two skills essential to network management. "Traditionally, our folks [National Park Service employees] have felt comfortable in their own kingdom; they feel less comfortable networking with the outside world," explains O'Neill. He is working to change this mind-set at Golden Gate. In fact, he is trying to transform altogether what it means to be a park service employee. "It's an entirely different role for public employees," explains O'Neill. "Rather than see themselves as doers, we try to get our people to see themselves as facilitators, conveners, and brokers of how to engage the community's talents to get our work accomplished."

The Department of the Interior has called the Golden Gate National Recreational Area the "archetype of a national park in the 21st Century." But GGNRA represents something more: a microcosm of the broader shift in governance around the globe. Its heavy reliance on partnerships, philosophy of leveraging nongovernmental organizations to enhance public value, and varied and innovative business relationships are all hallmarks of these shifts. Governments working in this new model rely less on public employees in traditional roles and more on a web of partnerships, contracts, and alliances to do the public's work. We call this development "governing by network." In this book we examine what this means, how it is changing the shape of the public sector, and how to manage a government in which achieving policy goals increasingly depends less on what public officials produce themselves and more on how they engage and manage external partners.

New Challenges, New Governance Model

In the twentieth century, hierarchical government bureaucracy was the predominant organizational model used to deliver public services and fulfill public policy goals. Public managers won acclaim by ordering those under them to accomplish highly routine, albeit professional, tasks with uniformity but without discretion. Today, increasingly complex societies force public officials to develop new models of governance.[2]

In many ways, twenty-first century challenges and the means of addressing them are more numerous and complex than ever before. Problems have become both more global and more local as power disperses and boundaries (when they exist at all) become more fluid. One-size-fits-all solutions have given way to customized approaches as the complicated problems of diverse and mobile populations increasingly defy simplistic solutions.

The traditional, hierarchical model of government simply does not meet the demands of this complex, rapidly changing age. Rigid bureaucratic systems that operate with command-and-control procedures, narrow work restrictions, and inward-looking cultures and operational models are particularly ill-suited to addressing problems that often transcend organizational boundaries.

Consider homeland security. Acting alone, neither the Federal Bureau of Investigation nor the Central Intelligence Agency can effectively stop terrorists. These agencies require the assistance of a law enforcement network that crosses agencies and levels of government. They need communications systems to capture, analyze, transform, and act upon information across public and private organizations at a speed, cost, and level that were previously impossible. Similarly, the Centers for Disease Control and Prevention cannot adequately respond to an outbreak of anthrax, smallpox, or other bioterrorism incident on its own. An effective response would require the activation of robust public health and emergency responder networks.

The hierarchical model of government persists, but its influence is steadily waning, pushed by governments' appetite to solve ever more complicated problems and pulled by new tools that allow innovators to fashion creative responses. This push and pull is gradually producing a new model of government in which executives' core responsibilities no longer center on managing people and programs but on organizing resources, often belonging to others, to produce public value. Government agencies, bureaus, divisions, and offices are becoming less important as direct service providers, but more important as generators of public value within the web of multiorganizational, multigovernmental, and multisectoral relationships that increasingly characterize modern government. "[W]hat exists in most spheres of policy is a dense mosaic of policy tools, many of them placing public agencies in complex, interdependent relationships with a host of third-party partners," explains Lester Salamon, author of several books on the role of nonprofits in public service delivery.[3] Thus government by network bears less resemblance to a traditional organizational chart than it does to a more dynamic web of computer networks that can organize or reorganize, expand or contract, depending on the problem at hand.

Networks can serve a range of impromptu purposes, such as creating a marketplace of new ideas inside a bureaucracy or fostering cooperation between colleagues. We use the term in this book, however, in reference to initiatives deliberately undertaken by government to accomplish public goals, with measurable performance goals, assigned responsibilities to each partner, and structured information flow. The ultimate goal of these efforts is to produce the maximum possible public value, greater than the sum of what each lone player could accomplish without collaboration. Public-private networks come in many forms, from ad hoc networks that are activated only intermittently—often in response to a disaster—to channel partnerships in which governments use private firms and nonprofits to serve as distribution channels for public services and transactions.

In a world in which elusive, decentralized, nonstate entities like al Qaeda, Hezbollah, and narcotic-trafficking cartels represent the biggest threat to Western democracies, the networked approach has become critical to national security. As RAND analysts John Arquilla and Dave Ronfeldt explain: "It takes a network to fight a network."[4] Government alone, for example, cannot thwart cyber attacks on telephone systems, power grids, financial systems, dams, municipal water systems, and the rest of our nation's critical infrastructure. Why? The private sector owns between 85 and 90 percent of the infrastructure. Recognizing this, the federal government has formed several multisectoral networks to coordinate cyber-security efforts. The government and private sector have established private computer networks that allow private industry and government to share information and remain in contact in the event of a large cyber attack. These networks, Information Sharing and Analysis Centers, exist in the financial, telecommunications, chemical, transportation, food, energy, water and information technology sectors.[5]

This networked model for combating cyber terrorism demonstrates the extent to which government is changing in response to today's more complicated problems. In simpler times the federal government might have employed a command-and-control approach for such a critical initiative. But in the wake of the September 11th terrorist attacks, a centralized approach was neither feasible nor desirable. As President George W. Bush explained when unveiling his federal cyber-security initiative: "The cornerstone of America's cyberspace security strategy is and will remain a public-private partnership. . . . Only by acting together can we build a more secure future in cyberspace."

The Rise of Government by Network

Historically governments have collaborated extensively with private firms, associations, and charitable organizations to accomplish public goals and deliver services. The ancient Greeks, for example, outsourced tax collection to tax farmers and leased out the state's mines to concessionaires.[6] However, thanks to a variety of factors, including advances in technology and the broader changes in the economy and society that favor networked forms of organization, today's networked government trend is both greater in breadth and different in kind than anything seen previously. In particular, governance by network represents the confluence of four influential trends that are altering the shape of public sectors worldwide.

▲ *Third-party government:* the decades-long increase in using private firms and nonprofit organizations—as opposed to government employees—to deliver services and fulfill policy goals.

▲ *Joined-up government:* the increasing tendency for multiple government agencies, sometimes even at multiple levels of government, to join together to provide integrated service.

▲ *The digital revolution:* the recent technological advances that enable organizations to collaborate in real time with external partners in ways previously not possible.

▲ *Consumer demand:* increased citizen demand for more control over their own lives and more choices and varieties in their government services, to match the customized service provision technology has spawned in the private sector.

Growth of Third-Party Government

This book focuses on situations where government officials intentionally engage networks of providers to enhance the delivery of public goods. These relationships are typically more complex than simple government-to-vendor outsourcing, but their roots nevertheless emanate from the varied and increased growth of third-party government, which is transforming the public sector from a service provider to a service facilitator.[7] We concentrate here, however, more on those networks that require ongoing public leadership and management. Third-party service delivery models—contracts between government agencies, commercialization, public-private partnerships, outsourcing, concession arrangements, and privatization—are a central component of the trend toward networked governing. New Deal–style initiatives, in which government assumes the dominant service delivery role, have become increasingly rare, especially for newly developed programs. As University of Pennsylvania professor Donald Kettl notes: "Every major policy initiative launched by the federal government since World War II—including Medicare and Medicaid, environmental cleanup and restoration, antipoverty programs and job training, interstate highways and sewage treatment plants—has been managed through public-private partnerships."[8]

This shift is particularly apparent in the area of service contracting. Between 1990 and 2001, federal-level contracting jumped by 24 percent in real terms.[9] (This increase is more remarkable considering the huge defense cutbacks resulting from the end of the cold war.) According to Paul Light of the Brookings Institution, federal contractors outnumbered federal employees by more than two to one and contract-generated federal jobs soared by more than 700,000 between 1999 and 2002. During the same period, the number of civil service employees actually fell by 50,000.[10] In fact, the federal government now spends about $100 billion more annually for contracts than it does for employee salaries.[11]

Similar shifts are under way in state and local government as well. According to the Government Contracting Institute, state government contracts to private firms rose 65 percent between 1996 and 2001, reaching a total of $400 billion.[12] Contracting now consumes about 19 percent of state operating budgets, and when state-delivered Medicaid benefits are included, the percentage goes even higher.[13]

Third-party delivery models are increasing found not only in long-established areas such as information technology, trash collection, and social services but also in many nontraditional sectors. In the United States, the Netherlands, and the United Kingdom, for example, dozens of school authorities have contracted with the private sector not only to build and modernize their schools, but also to operate them. As a result, delivering education services and managing schools has become big business. The number of for-profit companies managing public schools grew by 70 percent in 2001 in the United States. One of the largest education service firms, the Edison Project, opened its first school in 1995 and now operates 130 public schools that serve approximately 132,000 students in twenty states.

Prison administration is another area in which third-party service delivery has soared recently. In 1990 private correctional facilities worldwide housed only 15,300 prisoners. By 2000 this number had reached 145,160—an 849 percent increase in a single decade.[14] In the United States 158 private correctional facilities now operate in thirty states, Puerto Rico, and the District of Columbia. Texas leads this trend, with as many private prisons as the next three states combined.

Private contractors have even become an integral component of warfare. Since 1991 the number of active duty troops in the United States

Army has plummeted by 32 percent—from 711,000 to 487,000. Private companies have taken up much of the slack, carrying out many tasks formerly reserved for soldiers.[15] Indeed, when nations go to war, armed forces rely increasingly on private military support firms to establish communications systems, coordinate logistics, and maintain bases. Approximately 8 percent of the Pentagon's overall budget is spent on contracts with such firms. This number does not include contracting costs incurred in the Iraq War.

Even more striking is the role played by the approximately 1,000 private military companies involved in nearly every component of warfare—from training soldiers to transporting armed vehicles into war zones to simulating war games.[16] Explains Paul Lombardi, chief executive officer of Northern Virginia–based DynCorp International, which provided armed security for Afghanistan president Hamid Karzai following the October 2002 war in Afghanistan: "You could fight without us, but it would be difficult. Because we're so involved, it's difficult to extricate us from the process."[17]

Nowhere has the increased reliance on private contractors and military companies been more apparent than in Iraq, both during the war and the reconstruction efforts. In the 1991 Gulf War, there was one contractor for every fifty to one hundred soldiers. By 2003, when the United States invaded Iraq, the ratio of contractors to soldiers was down to one to ten.[18] The U.S. government hired contractors to do every kind of task imaginable, from maintaining military planes and cooking soldiers' food to training the new Iraqi army and police forces and even interrogating prisoners.[19] Dozens of contractors were killed in Iraq in 2003 and 2004 performing these duties. "The military and the civilian-contractor role are exactly the same," said Mel Goudie, the former director of the Baghdad Police Academy and an official with the U.S. Coalition Provisional Authority.[20]

The unprecedented use of contractors in Iraq became a lightning rod for criticism. Allegations ranged from favoritism in awarding contracts for reconstruction to excessive profits to a general lack of accountability of contractors after charges that at least one may have allowed, or encouraged, soldiers to abuse prisoners at the infamous Abu Ghraib prison in Baghdad.

Brookings Institution scholar Peter W. Singer, author of *Corporate Warriors: The Rise of the Privatized Military Industry,* cites three major reasons for the rapid rise of contractors on the battlefield.[21] First, the global military downsizing has created a labor pool of more than 6 million recently released or retired soldiers just as the number of violent conflicts around the world has increased. Second, warfare has become more dependent on extremely sophisticated technology systems, increasing military reliance on civilian specialists who can operate these highly complex systems. Third, Singer believes this rise reflects the broader privatization movement that has swept much of the world since the 1980s. We would add a fourth reason: private companies have become increasingly skilled at managing sprawling, complicated logistics chains (that is, networks), and by using these sophisticated private integrators, the military has been able to enhance its core war-making function.

However one feels about this development—and there are good arguments on both sides—the fact of the matter is that the line between military personnel and contractors during war has become blurred. "I'm not sure there is a line," says retired major general Edward B. Atkeson, "It's at the edge of a cloud and we've been fading into it and we're still trying to determine how far we want to go."[22]

Less spectacularly, governments also rely increasingly on private firms and nonprofits to deliver varied resource management and environmental services. Private companies across the country manage nearly 70 percent of waste tonnage generated in the United States and own more than 53 percent of its solid waste facilities.[23] Countless environmental public-private partnerships are also flourishing across the country. In Texas, for example, where 87 percent of the land is privately held, the state has entered into public-private partnerships with hundreds of landowners to conserve and restore open space and wildlife habitat. On the global front, New Zealand has privatized its forests and fisheries, while in Africa several entities have formed the Congo Basin Forest Partnership, which aims to combat illegal logging and enforce antipoaching laws.[24] Partners include twelve countries, scores of nongovernmental organizations such as Conservation International and the World Wildlife Fund, various private companies, and a host of government agencies.[25]

Private firms and nonprofit organizations also play an integral role in moving citizens from welfare to work. Thanks to the landmark 1996 welfare reform law, states have enormous freedom to contract with nonprofits, private companies, and religious organizations for wefare-to-work service delivery. Dozens of counties—including Palm Beach in Florida, San Diego in California, and Hennepin in Minnesota—responded by creating public-private welfare-to-work networks. The most far-reaching of these networks is in Wisconsin. In Milwaukee a welfare recipient can use most of the social service system without encountering a single public employee. In all, state and local governments spend more than $1.5 billion a year—13 percent of federal and state maintenance-of-effort expenditures—on private contracts for welfare-to-work-related services.[26]

A similar trend is under way in child welfare. Arizona, Florida, Kansas, Michigan, and Ohio have outsourced all or part of child welfare service delivery to the private sector. In Florida community-based non-profits now run the child welfare systems in dozens of counties, and the state's entire child welfare system is slated for eventual privatization. In Kansas a network of nonprofit and for-profit providers has delivered all foster care and adoption services statewide since 1997.

In the United Kingdom as well, government increasingly uses non-governmental entities to deliver social services. In 1980 government agencies in Great Britain delivered the overwhelming majority of social services in that country. Only 14 percent were provided by private firms or voluntary organizations. Less than two decades later, however, that number had jumped to 40 percent.[27] "The distinctions between public and private are eroding rapidly," says David Henshaw, chief executive of the Liverpool City Council in the United Kingdom. "As these boundaries crumble . . . collaborative joint venture partnerships, where partners focus on outcomes, success, and solutions, are inevitably the future."

The public sector outsourcing trend shows no signs of abating. In fact, governments are likely to respond to two other major developments of this decade—the giant baby-boomer retirement wave that will soon hit the public sector workforce and fiscal limitations that require more for less from government—by relying even more on outside partners in coming years than they do today.

Joined-Up Government

Of course, outsourcing alone cannot cure the problems of hierarchical government. When a narrowly focused, inward-looking government bureaucracy contracts a service to a private company, citizens still receive the service through a narrow, isolated channel, and dealing with four contractors, for example, is not much of an improvement over interacting with four government agencies.

This problem has led to the second trend driving the growth of networked government: the joining up of various levels and agencies of government to provide more integrated services. Often referred to in the United Kingdom and elsewhere as "joined-up government," this reform entails dismantling the stovepipes so prevalent in hierarchical government and enabling agencies to better share information and coordinate their efforts. Success in this area is critical to improving much of what government does today—from fighting the war on terrorism to meeting complex environmental challenges.

Joined-up government is the signature component of British prime minister Tony Blair's modernization program. "Many of the biggest challenges facing government do not fit easily into traditional Whitehall [United Kingdom government] structures . . . ," Blair has explained. "We need better coordination and more teamwork right across government if, for example, we are to meet the skills and educational challenges of the new century or achieve our aim of eliminating child poverty within twenty years."[28] One of dozens of the Blair administration's recent joined-up efforts is an initiative to reduce social exclusion by reintegrating those who have "fallen through the cracks" into society.[29] The agency established to coordinate the effort includes representatives from ministries such as Education, Environment, Transport, and Health.[30] According to the Blair government, since the initiative was launched in 1997, fewer people sleep on the streets and fewer children drop out of school.

Australia has also undertaken a host of integrated service efforts. The largest, Centrelink, is an ambitious project that draws together under one roof a variety of social services from eight different federal departments as well as from various state and territorial governments. The goal is to offer one-stop shopping across a variety of services for citizens.

Joined-up government efforts are also burgeoning across the United States. For example, Oregon's "No Wrong Door" initiative operates on the principle that citizens seeking state-level human services should be able to access help from the first point of government contact—regardless of which agency they contact. Oregon's new, integrated human services model replaces its previous, fragmented structure that required clients to deal with up to five networks of field offices, multiple case workers, and multiple case plans to obtain services. Under the new model, the five networks of field offices have been reduced to one integrated network.

At the federal level, joined-up government is seen in the Bush administration's twenty-four cross-agency, cross-government e-government projects. Each initiative—whether campground reservations or business registration—involves multiple agencies, and some efforts even incorporate multiple levels of government. For example, the Business Gateway, a Small Business Administration project that reduces paperwork for businesses, involves both state and local governments. This collaboration meets one of the Business Gateway's goals: small firms should be able to complete their paperwork once, in one place, rather than reporting the same information to multiple levels of government. For instance, today a trucker interested in operating a rig may be required to complete up to thirty-eight forms from a jumble of federal and state agencies. According to the trucking industry, such red tape costs the average trucker about $500 in lost time. To streamline this process, the Business Gateway, the Department of Transportation, and the trucking industry are working to standardize federal and state filing requirements. They are also working to employ interactive "smart" forms and Wizard tools in the reporting program. The goal? Allow truckers to submit their information one time and in one place.

Some of the United States' most ambitious joined-up efforts are unfolding in federal and state homeland security. Such innovations have been prompted by post–September 11 revelations that better information sharing and better interagency collaboration might have prevented the attacks on the Pentagon and the World Trade Center. Many states, for example, have developed sophisticated information systems to break down the walls between territorial law enforcement agencies. Colorado's Integrated Justice Information Network links five state-level criminal justice agencies—law enforcement, prosecution, courts, adult corrections, and juvenile corrections—to create one virtual criminal justice information system.

The Digital Revolution

Back in the 1930s an economist named Ronald Coase was trying to figure out what explained the rise of huge, modern corporations when he hit upon a unique insight—one which eventually landed him the Nobel Prize. Coase posited that the size of organizations is determined by the cost of gathering information. Large business organizations developed, he said, because of the transaction costs involved in creating, selling, and distributing goods and services.[31] Firms exist to minimize these transaction costs. The higher the transaction costs of performing a given function, the more likely the organization was to do that function itself, rather than contracting with another firm to perform it. At the time of Coase's observations, the transaction costs of doing business between organizations were generally extraordinarily high—information and supplies both moved at a glacial pace. As a result companies chose to produce many goods themselves, rather than contracting with outside companies. In so doing, they built massive, hierarchical structures to gather, process, certify, and store all the information they needed to take orders, make products, ship goods, and sell to customers. Coase's theories helped to explain the growth of hierarchical bureaucracy in government and in the private sector in the first half of the twentieth century.[32]

Now the Internet has reduced the cost of information to a fraction of what it once was. Along with e-mail and other communications technologies, the Internet has made communicating and collaborating with partners across organizational boundaries infinitely better, faster, and cheaper. The traditional costs of partnering such as travel, meetings, document exchange, and communications—all very real and often very large—have dropped by many orders of magnitude. Modern technologies allow organizations to share data and integrate their business processes with partners outside the four walls of the organization, enabling them to share information in real time about supply and demand and customers' preferences. The Dell Computer Corporation illustrates this change. The company shares production scheduling, demand forecasts, and other information with its suppliers electronically, allowing Dell to respond more quickly to changing customer needs and eliminate the need to stockpile weeks of inventory. Moreover many of the company's routine transactions with its partners have been automated, thereby further driving down the transaction costs of collaboration. The result of these and other innovations? As Coase predicted: more partnerships, more alliances, and more outsourcing as it increasingly becomes more cost efficient for organizations to partner than to do certain tasks themselves.[33] "It [the New Economy] enables you to have more specialization and greater production, because you're more efficient," Coase said decades later in 2000. "You'll get more small firms as a result, but large firms will also get larger, because they can concentrate on core activities and contract out what they can't do well."[34]

As the Dell example demonstrates, the digital revolution has also enabled complex systems to be organized in new and different ways. These technological advances strongly favor networked organizational forms. The U.S. military, faced with fighting far-flung networks of terrorist cells, is exploring the development of networked approaches in all facets of warfare.[35] For example, the Pentagon's Joint Forces Command is experimenting with ending the practice of setting up large battlefield headquarters, opting instead to send only a small staff into war zones. This group would use information technology to tap into a network of specialized civilian, military, and contractor expertise back on the home front. Such an approach simply would not have been possible two decades ago.

Citizen Choice

Citizens today expect to be able to buy goods through multiple channels, both retail and e-tail. And despite the growing size of large private corporations, consumers expect more control over their choices. They want to tell the manufacturer what color and options they prefer. Dell leads its customers through dozens of online options to configure a new laptop. Music services track what their customers listen to and send them music closer to their tastes. Mass commercial customization has made consumers less tolerant of going to an official motor vehicle license branch some distance from their house and waiting in line for mediocre service.

People in need of social services want the ability to configure how and when they secure help.

In his inaugural address President George W. Bush called for a nation of "citizens, not spectators; citizens, not subjects." Engaged citizens accept responsibility and participate in the marketplace and in civic affairs, but they also do not sit meekly at the bottom of hierarchical delivery systems waiting for the delivery of undifferentiated products. Responding to choice demands a different model of government. The more important that variety and customization becomes in service delivery, the more networks will be the preferred delivery form.

Wired, Joined-Up, and Pushed Down

Governing by network represents the synthesis of these four trends, combining the high level of public-private collaboration characteristic of third-party government with the robust network management capabilities of joined-up government, and then using technology to connect the network together (figure 1-1) and give citizens more choices in service delivery options.

This synthesis is seen in the way that the city of Birmingham, England, delivers drug and alcohol treatment services. Birmingham officials discovered that different city agencies received treatment funding from several central government agencies, meaning that each agency operated its own treatment programs and negotiated its own contracts with community providers. "We had to break out of the silos created by the dedicated funding streams," says Jamie Morris of the Birmingham Public Safety Partnership. The city accomplished this by pooling all treatment funding appropriated by the central government. It then created a joint commissioning group—composed of representatives from each agency—to oversee the fund and negotiate contracts with the providers that would actually deliver the services. The result? A government network that manages a network of nonprofit and for-profit providers.

As is the case in Birmingham, the most complex networks often exist when government is horizontally joined up and the delivery of services is vertically pushed down. Local governments often face interrelated, seemingly intractable, problems—youth crime, teenage pregnancy, drug abuse,

FIGURE 1.1   Models of Government

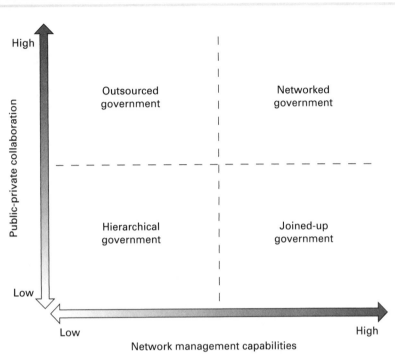

lack of affordable housing. To address these, governments often weave together networks of solutions and then push the delivery down to community groups. In Indianapolis, for example, public health, public housing, and community policing groups joined community development and neighborhood leaders to develop and deliver a wide range of regenerative services to long-neglected neighborhoods.[36] The city combined funding from the U.S. Department of Housing and Urban Development and the U.S. Department of Labor with local public health, infrastructure, and philanthropic investments to produce a broad network of connected, customer-responsive community services. The various levels of government did not actually *deliver* a single service in this model—all were delivered by private and nonprofit entities.

These complex public-private, network-to-network collaboration models operate, with varying degrees of success, in nearly every area of public policy. The building of the National Aeronautics and Space Administration (NASA) Jim Webb Space Telescope, for example, involves multiple governments (the Germans are supplying many of the instruments; the French, the launch vehicle), multiple contractors (Northrop Grumman is the prime contractor), and several universities as well as NASA's in-house capabilities (the agency is doing the testing itself). Medicaid is a federal-state program in which health care services are delivered by private and nonprofit organizations, while a third party processes claims. Likewise, most job training programs, funded at least partially by federal and state governments, are administered by local workforce boards and delivered by networks of private and nonprofit providers. At the state level, Wisconsin's welfare delivery model engages multiple levels of government, multiple state agencies, a handful of nonprofit and for-profit administrators, and dozens of community-based subcontractors. At the municipal level, twelve local authorities in Manchester, England, joined up to procure from private and nonprofit providers placement services for adults and children with special care or educational needs. In short, as governments confront increasingly complex problems and technology facilitates more sophisticated responses, government's use of third-party public service delivery models also grows in complexity.

Indeed, discussions about government innovation rarely center on outsourcing versus bureaucracy anymore. The pressing question has become how to manage diverse webs of relationships in order to create value.

Management Challenges

As government relies more and more on third parties to deliver services, its performance depends ever more on its ability to manage partnerships and to hold its partners accountable.[37] For example, NASA and the U.S. Department of Energy both spend more than 80 percent of their respective budgets on contracts. The Department of Energy has only 16,000 employees; contractors at the agency outnumber employees by more than 130,000 people. These two agencies have become de facto contract management agencies. For NASA, the Department of Energy, and a growing number of other agencies at all levels of government around the globe, the skill with which the agency manages networks contributes as much to its successes and failures as the skill with which it manages its own public employees. This development has prompted some critics to coin the term "hollow state," referring to a government with little or no capacity to manage its partners, let alone deliver services itself.[38]

We believe that governments can in many instances produce more public value through a networked approach than they can through hierarchical methods, but we also recognize the enormous challenges associated with implementing this new model.[39] Some of these risks relate to structure and deal making. When a public official like the National Park Service's Brian O'Neill resorts to a network as a means to attract private uses and private finances, he must ensure that the more generalized public purpose is protected and that the private participation is congruent with and enhances those uses.

The second problem is managerial. As John Donahue, author of *The Privatization Decision,* told us: "Governing by network is hard, really hard. There are countless ways it can go wrong." One big obstacle: government's organizational, management, and personnel systems were designed to operate within a hierarchical, not a networked, model of government, and the two approaches often clash. Managing a portfolio of provider networks is infinitely different than managing divisions of employees. It requires a form of public management very different from what governments and their citizens have become accustomed to over the past hundred years. Government cannot through partnerships avoid its ultimate responsibility to the public for both the quality of a service and whether it is justly delivered. The problems of Iraqi prisoner abuse, for example, are every bit the problem of the Pentagon, whether they are committed by private contractors or by U.S. military personnel.

Unfortunately there are very few places for public officials to turn to learn more about managing networks. They have few guideposts to help them determine how they should use a network of providers to enhance value or how authority or money can help them set a network in motion. Guidance on issues as varied as whom to invite to the table or what level of government oversight is appropriate for a specific function are simply not addressed. In short, with some notable exceptions, current public management theory lags behind the practice of government by network.

This is not to say that there isn't a rich body of literature exploring issues around hierarchies, bureaucracies, and networks in the public sector.[40] A number of top-notch academics have made a career of analyzing government's use of networks, while the literature on how the public sector should organize the delivery of services includes classic tomes such as Max Weber's *Theory of Social and Economic Organization,* Oliver Williamson's *Markets and Hierarchies,* and James Q. Wilson's *Bureaucracy.*[41] These and other essential books on the subject have greatly informed our thinking, but missing from the growing body of work on networks and government is a practical guide, based on real-life lessons, on how to govern a public sector that does less and less itself.

Governing by Network aims to help fill this void and to facilitate debate and discussion on this important transformation. We have deliberately steered away from getting into an ideological argument about privatization in this book. Both of us have been intimately involved in this debate for many years.[42] But it is a debate that has grown stale. It simply does not reflect the reality of a world in which public and private boundaries are becoming increasingly blurred and governments of all ideological bents are partnering with private companies and nonprofit organizations to do more and more of the government's work.[43] As the networked approach to governance proliferates, polarized and simplistic debates about the pros and cons of contracting out government services are becoming increasingly irrelevant. More important is learning how to *manage* a government composed more and more of networks instead of people and programs. Exploring this issue is the main purpose of this book.

Governing by Network is divided into two major parts. Part one explains why networked governance is on the rise and addresses the myriad challenges government officials face when implementing this new model. Part two provides a framework as well as a set of tools for managing it.

CHAPTER 1—THE BOTTOM LINE

KEY POINTS

▲ The era of hierarchical government bureaucracy is coming to an end. Emerging in its place is a fundamentally different model—governing by network—in which government executives redefine their core responsibilities from managing people and programs to coordinating resources for producing public value.

▲ Governing by network represents the confluence of four trends that are altering the shape of public sectors worldwide:
  1. The rise in the use of private firms and nonprofits to do government's work,
  2. Efforts to "join up" governments horizontally and vertically to streamline processes from the perspective of the customer-citizen,
  3. Technological breakthroughs that dramatically reduce the costs of partnering, and
  4. Increased citizen demands for more choices in public services.

▲ As governments rely less on public employees and more on a web of partnerships and contracts to do the public's work, how well an agency manages networks contributes as much to its successes and failures as how well it manages its own public employees.

PITFALLS

▲ Changing the way goods and services are produced without changing the structure of government.

▲ Getting mired in the stale debate of whether contracting out is good or bad and ignoring the more important question of how to *manage* a government that does less and less itself.

TIPS

▲ Don't underestimate the management challenges of governing by network.

▲ Don't try to use traditional hierarchical controls to manage a horizontal government. Networked government requires a form of public management different from what the country has become accustomed to over the past 100 years.

EXAMPLES

▲ *The Golden Gate National Recreation Area.* This national park relies so heavily on partners to do everything from maintain historic buildings to rehabilitate stranded marine mammals that National Park Service employees constitute only 18 percent of its total workforce.

▲ *Iraq War and the U.S. Military.* Contractors have become an integral component of warfare, even on the battleground. During the Iraq War, there was one contractor for every ten soldiers.

TWO

Advantages of
the Network Model

Enacted by a Republican Congress, signed into law by a Democratic
president, and implemented by governors of both parties, the 1996
welfare reform bill was widely viewed as a great public policy success of the 1990s. And no state was more successful in moving from
the old cash-based welfare system to the new work-based support program than Wisconsin, where welfare caseloads plummeted 89 percent
between 1993 and 2000, and the poverty rate for single-parent families
fell from 30 percent to 25 percent between 1997 and 1999.[1]

At the heart of Wisconsin Works (W-2), the state's much heralded welfare reform program, was a fundamental shift in mission. Instead of simply dispensing cash benefits to welfare recipients, governments began to
help families achieve economic self-sufficiency. Administrative entitlements were out; work requirements, job training, transportation assistance, and time limits were in.

Although less well known, far-reaching management changes comple-
mented this shift in mission. Responsibility for operating the program
devolved to seventy-two W-2 agencies scattered across Wisconsin. These
entities, operated in some places by government officials and in others by
private providers, were each paid a flat fee and allocated a significant level
of operational freedom. In exchange for this flexibility, each W-2 agency
agreed to a set of rigorous, state-administered performance criteria.

Not only did Wisconsin's Department of Workforce Development refocus its mission and redefine its management responsibilities, but it also ended the county monopoly on program administration, opening the system to bids from private providers. Wisconsin's unprecedented approach continued to evolve; today, more than 70 percent of Wisconsin's W-2 workload is handled by private providers.

Milwaukee presents the most stunning example, with all five W-2 agencies being private organizations—four nonprofits and one for-profit firm. Dozens of local, community-based organizations support the W-2 agencies, providing a host of client services that range from job training to day care. The result is a complex but integrated welfare-to-work service delivery system made up almost wholly of private and nongovernmental organizations (figure 2-1).

Why did Wisconsin officials adopt a new welfare mission and pursue such a radically different delivery model in Milwaukee? Simple. Milwaukee's hierarchical, county-run system could administer the rules for determining whether in the old system a person qualified for benefits, but it was unequipped for the new complex challenges posed by welfare reform. Explains Jason Turner, the hard-charging former administrator of Wisconsin's W-2 program,

> There was no evidence that Milwaukee County was a capable public assistance manager. The component elements of a good welfare system are control of the client at all points in the system, a reduced number of moving parts—which means limiting the number of offices a client has to visit—short periods of time between different program components, and swift and sure sanctions. None of these applied in Milwaukee.[2]

Turner and the other Milwaukee architects believed that a networked service delivery model would offer significant advantages over the hierarchical system. For example, the devolved and privatized Milwaukee model enabled W-2 to access the community ties and specialized skills of dozens of local providers. These local groups offered a broader array of services tailored to client needs and circumstances than the county could, and this made-to-order approach encouraged more innovation than the standard, one-size-fits-all governmental model. "We wanted to

FIGURE 2.1 Wisconsin W-2 Network Delivery Model

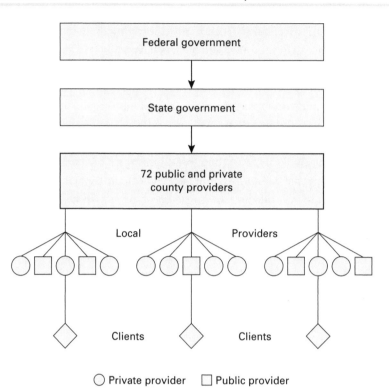

be able to look at different approaches, to really test what was the best way to deliver services," says Jennifer Alexander, the former director of Wisconsin's Division of Workforce Development. "Some providers had unique ways of making food stamps available; others had unique approaches to job assessment."

YW Works, an enterprise of the local YWCA, was one Milwaukee provider that carefully tailored its services to client needs and circumstances. Its 114-year history of working with local women placed it in a unique position to move welfare recipients—the vast majority of whom were women—into the world of work. For example, before a woman enters a skill-based work training program, YW Works conducts a comprehensive analysis of her soft skills, such as interviewing for a job and arriving for work on time. "We deal with women holistically, with where they are in their lives, from the time they enter, to the time they leave the program," explains Rita Riner, the vice president of YW Works.

The Milwaukee model also offers more flexibility than traditional, government service delivery models. Providers have a considerable amount of freedom to adapt their delivery models to meet shifting circumstances and needs. "We're constantly changing our strategy as our population changes . . . and as our employers change what they're looking for," explains an executive at another W-2 provider. "I always tell people here that our program is a work in progress."

Wisconsin's W-2 is one of the most sophisticated networked government programs that we studied. It illustrates both the tremendous promise and the myriad complexities of government by network. This chapter examines the benefits of networked governance. A handful of benefits, in particular, have been particularly powerful drivers of the movement to networks: specialization, innovation, speed, flexibility, and increased reach. These successes bring with them challenges that we address in chapter three.

Specialization

The networked organizational model is becoming the defining feature of business in the twenty-first century, fundamentally altering the structure and operation of many companies. Networks are usurping the hierarchical model in companies and industries ranging from health care to information technology. "In some industries the production network is the most important unit of competition . . . ," writes Jeffrey H. Dyer in *Collaborative Advantage: Winning through Extended Enterprise Supplier Networks*. "Firms are achieving competitive success only when they assemble a network of firms that know how to collaborate effectively to create unique, valuable, and difficult-to-imitate products and services."[3] In the health care industry, large national players have increasingly partnered with local providers to form integrated service delivery models by using managerial and marketing expertise to reduce administrative and overhead costs while increasing volume and revenues. Local providers, for their part, serve as the customer touch point and offer deep knowledge of the local market.

The growth of the networked model is being driven by a host of advantages it offers to both business and government over traditional hierarchical structures. One benefit is that networks free companies to concentrate on their core mission and exploit the expertise of "best of breed" providers. For example, the Porsche Boxster is wholly assembled by Valmet, a Finnish engineering firm that specializes in developing and manufacturing high-performance specialty cars. Valmet's reputation as the world's premier manufacturer of convertible systems is so solid that Porsche has given Valmet management of the Boxster's entire supply chain. That has freed Porsche to focus on its core competencies: designing new automobile models and maintaining and enhancing its brand image.

Porsche is not alone in adopting a networked business model and devoting its resources to specialization. Toyota relies on a vast network of suppliers and distribution channels to do everything from manufacturing auto chassis to managing logistics.[4] Software company Siebel Systems has built an "ecosystem" of alliance partners to carry out systems integration, consulting, and software and content development tasks. Cisco Systems owns only two of thirty plants that produce its products, and orders for Cisco routers and switches go directly to the company's contract manufacturers.

The advantages of specialization also drive the shift toward networked approaches to government. When Indianapolis outsourced its information technology operations, metropolitan airport, and wastewater treatment system to outside providers during the 1990s, the most important assets that the city secured in each case were the highly specialized technical knowledge and management talents of world-class operators.[5] For example, when BAA, the operator of Heathrow, Gatwick, and other major airports, assumed management of Indianapolis International Airport, it brought food, beverage, and retail services, as well as capital planning, financial, parking, facilities maintenance, and real estate development talent. The city, acting alone, could never have marshaled such stellar resources across so broad an array of subject matters.

Innovation

Because they enable government to explore a greater range of alternatives that involve a variety of providers, networks encourage the kind of experimentation so critical to the innovation process. To those who study how innovation develops, it should come as no surprise that winners of Harvard's Innovations in American Government award often represent programs that use network delivery models. In fact, innovation often faces higher hurdles in a hierarchical organization—particularly a government bureaucracy—than within networks, because a host of internal horizontal constraints tend to restrict the interaction necessary to develop good ideas and vertical barriers prevent the developed ideas from bubbling up to decision.[6]

Innovation played an important role in the United States victory in the cold war. The networks of private firms that built weapons systems for America were better able to adapt and innovate than hierarchical state-owned enterprises working under the Soviet Union's command-and-control model. To be sure, the military buildup brought with it real problems—the rise of the military-industrial complex and contracting fraud, to name just two—but difficulties notwithstanding, this networked approach was far more dynamic than its hierarchical counterpart. As Harvard professor Elaine Kamarck explains:

> Seeking ever better weapons against the Soviet Union, the United States engaged countless corporations, universities, and private laboratories, along with their own internal research laboratories, in developing sophisticated weaponry. In the kind of controlled experiment that rarely happens in the real world, the Soviet Union, a totalitarian state, kept its weapons research within the all-encompassing bureaucracy of the Communist state. By 1989 the experiment was over. . . . Government by network had won; bureaucratic government had lost.[7]

Similarly, the Manhattan Project's weblike organizational structure was intended to maximize the potential for innovation. Different companies and universities were given responsibility for producing the discrete components necessary to make the atomic bomb. The DuPont Corporation ran the plutonium project; Union Carbide developed gaseous diffusion; Chrysler produced diffusers; and the University of Wisconsin supplied electrostatic generators needed to measure nuclear constants. In some cases, Leslie Groves, the project manager, assigned the same task to several entities as an added competitive spur to innovation.[8]

Network delivery systems, when set up correctly, also produce another kind of innovation opportunity. Democratic governance should constantly produce higher-quality citizen services, and a key source of innovation comes in response to citizen reactions. These reactions are registered in increasingly proliferated ways: through call centers, on the World Wide Web, on the street to a public servant, in a neighborhood center, and so on. Hierarchical government tends to insulate middle and upper managers from these experiences. In contrast, a networked response typically increases the number of individuals working on governmental matters who experience these reactions. When supported by good communication and knowledge management tools, this expanded contact with the client leads to enhanced information about customer concerns and attitudes, which in turn boosts innovation and responsiveness, as well as spread successful practices more quickly.[9] In this way, networks foster learning and continuous improvement by providing more timely access to a broader knowledge base than is possible within a single organization.

Speed and Flexibility

Flexibility enhances the speed with which the government responds. Because of their hierarchical decision-making structure, inflexible bureaucracies tend to react slowly to new situations. The rigidity of government personnel and procurement systems makes it difficult to move quickly or change directions when circumstances warrant.

Networks, in contrast, tend to be more nimble and flexible than hierarchies.[10] They enable government to bypass stultifying procedures that slow personnel movement or the acquisition of urgent materials or partners. They also leverage both private sector and governmental funds. When circumstances change or performance lags, well-designed contracts allow for changes in terms or participants.[11] Networks permit more rapid—and usually less politically painful—downsizing and upsizing than does a hierarchy. The federal government used this "surge-tank" management model during two of its most important twentieth century initiatives: the Manhattan Project to develop the atomic bomb, and the race to be the first country to land a man on the moon.

During World War II, the United States and Germany engaged in a life-or-death struggle to be the first to build a nuclear weapon. There simply was not time for bureaucratic niceties. Instead, General Groves, the legendary Manhattan Project manager, threw out the rule book and built a far-flung network that brought together more than one dozen colleges and universities, two dozen corporate partners, and thousands of scientists at the federal Los Alamos laboratory. (He managed to do this while keeping the project's ultimate aim a complete secret.) This model was retained in the years following the war when the Soviet Union entered the arms race. In fact, of the 60,000 people employed by the Atomic Energy Commission in 1951, all but 5,000 were contractors.[12]

In the 1960s and 1970s the federal government employed the surge-tank model again during its cold war space race against the Soviet Union. In 1962, the year before President John F. Kennedy committed to landing a man on the moon, NASA employed 3,500 contractors and 23,000 civil servants.[13] Only two years later, in 1964, the Apollo program was running at full steam, and NASA had retained 10,000 service contractors to perform basic tasks; thousands more to manufacture rockets and vehicles; 69,000 contractor scientists and engineers to conduct research and development; and 32,000 civil servants.[14] After Neil Armstrong raised an American flag on the moon in 1969, NASA scaled back its program and quickly slashed the number of contractor scientists and engineers by 51,000.[15] Its own workforce, by contrast, fell by only 800 employees, demonstrating again the greater flexibility governments retain when they use contractors.

The advantages that government managers gain with such flexibility simply cannot be overemphasized. By using outside partners to deliver a service or accomplish a task, managers can hire, fire, assign, and reassign on short notice in a way that simply is not possible and will likely never be possible with public employees. David Chu, the Defense Department's personnel chief, explains: the civil service system is "not an attractive alternative. It's hard to work. . . . It's not responsive. You can't move people around."[16]

Networks also enable governments to increase productivity when new demands bump up against hiring limits. In recent years public managers have faced hiring freezes, employee caps, and governmentwide head-count limits—blunt tools designed to send a message that bureaucracy size must be contained. Federal, state, and local governments have used these tools extensively. In the 1990s, for example, the Texas legislature froze hiring, put ceilings on employment, eliminated vacant positions, and enacted across-the-board personnel reductions in successive legislative sessions. In the face of such restrictions, the Texas government sometimes engaged outside organizations to be able to meet new legislative mandates and surges in work without increasing the number of public employees. This surge capacity can be abused, however. In the past the federal government, from time to time, used contract employees not as a part of a designed network but simply to avoid head-count limits.

There is another important way in which networks can quickly produce flexible responses. In today's interconnected world, where multiple programs interact with multiple levels of government and millions of individuals, rigid, one-size-fits-all approaches cannot effectively solve complex policy problems such as reducing youth crime or rebuilding drug-infested communities.[17] Government must cultivate solutions that provide maximum client flexibility and that give substantial discretion to those providers closest to the problem or customer.

For example, a neighborhood center with multiple relationships can more adroitly direct a mother facing abuse, poverty, or other difficulties to appropriate shelter, counseling, or workforce training than can an agency devoted to delivering a single service. The networked center can engage the creativity and specialized skills of a range of providers while retaining the freedom to adjust the range of services offered as circumstances change. Moreover, it can do all this while maintaining its relationship with the mother and her family. In this way, networking can help government evolve from a one-size-fits-all service provider to a one-stop portal for myriad providers.

Finally, a local center that is part of a network is less limited by rigid government programmatic restrictions and therefore can also fill in funding gaps with private dollars, which generally have fewer restrictions than government funds. The local center can refer a mother to another provider without waiting for her to qualify for a federal or state program. The flexibility of the private provider allows a speedy, customized response to clients whose needs are continually changing.

Increased Reach

Government innovators must shop for necessary resources in order to increase the reach of their networks. Sometimes those resources are financial, and the need for private capital—or government dollars—draws other potential partners and their dollars. Or a government official may have an idea that requires specialized management talents unavailable without engaging partners. In the United States and the United Kingdom, for example, many local governments have entered into alliances with private companies and associations to promote local tourism and economic development in the belief that these organizations are more skilled at marketing.[18]

In other cases an innovator may face impossible investment hurdles because the government capital budget has been reduced. Networked approaches help government officials expand reach without incurring huge capital costs by requiring nongovernmental partners to provide (that is, finance) all startup capital. Sometimes to be financially feasible a project must be implemented on a larger scale. A medium-size city in a traditional bureaucratic model often misses best practices simply because of scale. Now, through participating in a network, a city can span geographical lines, sharing customers with other jurisdictions, benefiting from technology costs spread across a much larger base, reducing risks, and utilizing world-class experts. Thus the network can remove jurisdiction-imposed scale limitations. A small or medium-size city no longer needs to reject good ideas merely because of these hurdles; a network partner can provide an answer, take a risk, or reduce the marginal cost by attracting other government customers.

But increased reach also means using the network to connect more broadly to customers of government services. That was one of the main goals driving the Internal Revenue Service's (IRS) decision to partner with the private sector in its initiative to encourage more Americans to file their taxes online. In 1998 the 105th Congress—attempting to save money, expedite the refund process, and reduce American disgust with the IRS—mandated that 80 percent of all tax returns, or more than 120 million, should be filed electronically by 2007. Congressional appropriators believed that convincing the majority of Americans to file electronic returns was the only way to prevent huge federal outlays in the near future to deal with an increasing volume of tax returns. "Over the next decade, we'll need to process 40 million additional returns with no additional resources," said Terry Lutes, the deputy chief for information technology services at the IRS. "The only way to do that is [to get] at least 40 million more taxpayers to file electronically."

Although the case for online filing was never in doubt, congressionally driven goals were, at the least, quite ambitious. In 1998 only about 24 million returns—a fifth of the total—were filed electronically. Fully 70 percent of Americans were not even aware that they could file federal income tax returns online.

It did not take long for the IRS to realize that it would need massive assistance to meet congressional targets. It turned to the private sector and embarked on a plan to harness the technological and marketing prowess of tax software companies, national tax preparation firms, and tax accountants. "It was a no-brainer," explains Lutes. "Over half of all tax returns came in from tax professionals; millions more were completed by taxpayers with the help of tax software. We needed to work with the private sector to accomplish our goals."

Lutes hired a handful of national account managers—a job title virtually unheard of in government circles—and gave them a single goal: enlist software companies like Intuit, tax preparation firms like H&R Block and Jackson Hewitt, portals like AOL and MSN, individual practitioners, and banks and other financial institutions in the effort to shift tax return filing from paper to electronic format.

By 2002 the percentage of Americans aware of e-file had reached 80 percent and by 2004, more than 60 million returns, or about half of all tax returns filed by individuals, were sent in electronically.[19] Much of the increase was attributed to massive advertising campaigns from the agency's private sector partners. "They're a powerful ally in marketing the message of online filing," said Lutes.

Networks can also help governments expand their reach by enabling them to engage the nonprofit sector's innovative spirit and creativity in efforts to solve major social problems.[20] Infant mortality, high teen pregnancy rates, poor educational performance, drug abuse, and crime cannot be considered separately from the emotional and spiritual needs of

Government and the Nonprofit Sector:
An Increasingly Symbiotic Relationship

The nonprofit sector has grown dramatically in recent decades. It is bigger, more politically powerful, and more sophisticated than ever. Between 1977 and 1997, the number of new nonprofits averaged 23,000 a year—a growth rate much higher than that of private companies over the same period. (This growth accelerated in recent years, increasing from an average of 15,000 a year between 1977 and 1987 to more than 27,000 a year between 1987 and 1997.) One of every fifteen service jobs is found in the nonprofit sector.

Nonprofit revenue growth has also outpaced that of the private sector, rising 140 percent between 1977 and 1997 (after adjusting for inflation). This figure is nearly double the 81 percent growth rate of the U.S. economy over the same time period. Nonprofit revenue growth was especially robust in the arts, culture, social service, and health care fields. In each, the growth rate was at least double that of the broader economy.

As the nonprofit sector has grown, its funding from government sources has skyrocketed, rising 595 percent in real terms between 1977 and 1997. The percentage of nonprofit revenue received from government also rose—from 27 percent of total nonprofit revenues to 33 percent between 1977 and 1997. (When religious congregations are excluded from the definition of nonprofits, the government contributions to nonprofit revenues total 37 percent.) Again, the major beneficiaries of this increase were health, social service, and arts organizations, each of which saw its government support rise by 200 percent or more after adjusting for inflation.

The rise of the nonprofit sector means that governments now deliver less than half the social services that they finance. In most communities, three-fifths or more of health and social services are now delivered by either non-profit or for-profit providers. The result is an increasingly symbiotic relationship. Government is the largest funder of nonprofit organizations, which, in turn, deliver many health and social services to the poor, aged, and disabled on behalf of the state.

Source: Lester Salamon, *The Resilient Sector: The State of Nonprofit America* (Brookings, 2003), p. 51.

those who experience them. Nor can they be divorced from the need for personal responsibility. Government bureaucracies are ill equipped to solve such complicated problems, however, because their narrow programs are constrained by laws, rules, and regulations designed to prevent favoritism and ensure that everyone is treated alike.

Networks allow innovative government officials to discharge government's important role in solving social problems by supporting—not supplanting—functioning elements of civil society. Specifically, government can aid those in need by networking with and making funds more accessible to neighborhood and faith-based organizations that administer a proper and effective mix of service, love, and discipline. This approach empowers public innovators actively to bring disenfranchised citizens into the mainstream of American life through programs and policies that encourage citizens to be self-governing rather than passive receivers of government assistance and helpless victims of external social forces.

To maximize their potential, these networks often move both horizontally and vertically. Not only do they engage services across sectors, but they also employ the concepts of devolution that involve units of governments and programs that are closest to the customer. To be effective, networking calls for a fundamental shift in approach throughout government. Leaders and managers who have the authority, motivation, and vision to assess their situations and reshape the framework of their agencies will have to lead the way. And like any trailblazers, they are likely to encounter serious challenges of the kind explored in the next chapter.

CHAPTER 2—THE BOTTOM LINE

KEY POINTS

▲ Networks encourage the kind of experimentation so critical to the innovation process by enabling government to explore a greater range of alternatives involving a variety of providers.

▲ Networks also enable a government to concentrate on its core mission by leveraging the expertise of "best of breed" providers.

▲ Networks enhance flexibility. By using outside partners to deliver a service or accomplish a task, managers can increase, decrease, or change resources on short notice.

▲ The decentralized, fluid form of a network and the autonomy of each member allows for decisionmaking at the most appropriate level for the citizen.

TIPS

▲ Expand reach by engaging the nonprofit sector's innovative spirit and creativity in efforts to solve major social problems.

▲ Use networks when you need to expand rapidly—but only temporarily. In 1962 NASA employed 3,500 contractors. Only two years later, in 1964, the Apollo program was running at full steam, and NASA had retained 79,000 contractors. After the moon landing was accomplished, NASA was able to quickly ramp down its program, slashing the number of contractor scientists and engineers by 51,000.

EXAMPLES

▲ *Manhattan Project.* In its undertaking to build the atomic bomb, the U.S. government built a far-flung network that brought together more than one dozen colleges and universities, two dozen corporate partners, and thousands of scientists at the federal Los Alamos laboratory. In fact, of the 60,000 people employed by the Atomic Energy Commission after the bomb was dropped, all but 5,000 were contractors.

▲ *The IRS e-File Initiative.* To reach its goal of getting 80 percent of tax returns filed electronically, the IRS successfully formed innovative partnerships with private tax preparers and software manufacturers.

THREE

Challenges of the Network Model

I n chapter two we demonstrated the benefits Milwaukee achieved from using a networked model. What we did not talk about were the myriad challenges state officials encountered in implementing and managing such an extensive and complex provider network. Milwaukee officials early on faced the allegation that contractors misused state funds. One nonprofit provider was accused of using state funds to throw a party; another of using taxpayer dollars to lobby for a contract in another state. These problems, combined with issues of poor performance, forced Wisconsin to play a more active management role than it had anticipated upon launching Wisconsin Works. "We started seeing some patterns in W-2 providers where case management was not where it should have been," explained an official in the Division of Workforce Services. "This led to more intense monitoring on our part."

However, W-2 providers compiled their own set of complaints: the state reneged on its promises; the state overburdened them with mounds of paperwork; the state imposed unrealistic performance targets, and so on. Rita Riner of the YWCA expressed the frustration common among private providers: "The state changed some of the profit and performance standards on us in midstream, making it nearly impossible for us to reach their goals."

These are just a flavor of the issues Wisconsin officials confronted—most of them successfully—in the transition from a bureaucratic to a network model of service delivery. What Milwaukee's W-2 experience demonstrated above all else is that while the networked form of government offers marked advantages, it also poses a whole set of new management challenges for governments.[1] Successful networked management requires grappling with skill-set issues (managing a contract to capture value), technology issues (incompatible information systems), communications issues (one partner in the network, for example, might possess more information than another), and cultural issues (how interplay among various public, private, and non-profit sector cultures can create unproductive dissonance).

The first step in governing networks more effectively is having a thorough understanding of these and other challenges. Several examples in this book—the Department of Housing and Urban Development (HUD) HOPE VI program, profiled in the next chapter, for one—show how the same program administered differently can produce success or failure. Indeed, a program's success or failure often depends on whether the network manager masters the challenges of governing by network: aligning goals, providing oversight, averting communications meltdown, coordinating multiple partners, managing the tension between competition and collaboration, and overcoming data deficits and capacity shortages.

Goal Congruence

A supply-chain network might be constructed in the auto industry to build a car or truck or in the high-tech industry to build a computer or router. In either case, the metrics—price, timeliness, and quality—are relatively straightforward, and the end product is easy to define. If the network breaks down, it is usually possible to pinpoint the problem's location and fix it quickly. Participants in the commercial supply chain may, of course, disagree from time to time, but substantive differences regarding goals or values rarely arise among them.

Achieving goal congruence in the public sector is not so simple. Alignment of goals should mean congruence on outcomes, not processes. Government networks, however, tend to form to deliver the type of service whose outcomes are sometimes unclear, are difficult to measure, and may take years to realize. To complicate matters, networks often bring together actors whose goals simultaneously overlap and differ. Although government needs to hold its contractors accountable, the very complexity that necessitates a networked solution often makes the accountability process quite difficult. Actors in the network may be providing different services, all with narrow performance goals. For example, one provider may be narrowly rewarded based on whether a client finds a job; another may be rewarded based on whether the same client is no longer a victim of violence. Such varied criteria for success make for messy network management.

In addition, the missions of the organizations within the network do not always align well. Examples include networks, such as that involving La Bodega de Familia (see chapter four), that often involve a law enforcement partner whose mission to prevent crime through arrest may clash with those of a social service organization that focuses on treatment and rehabilitation.

Such tensions have surfaced in the HUD HOPE VI program, an initiative that makes large grants to city public housing authorities to replace units that are old, dense, and run down with units that better fit the character of the neighborhood. In turn, local public housing authorities contract out a wide range of related activities—from social services and counseling to development and construction. Tension sometimes develops between housing advocacy groups interested in making sure no existing tenants are displaced and community development officials more concerned with rebuilding neighborhoods, even if it means dispersing poor residents over a larger area. In many HOPE VI efforts, the contract partner responsible for mitigating tenant relocation has been at odds with community players or city officials who are more concerned with reducing the density of subsidized units to help revitalize the renewal.

Difficulty in aligning goals also appears in networks formed to address other thorny social issues such as teenage pregnancy. For example, a public agency interested in reducing teen pregnancy and deterring childbearing until marriage might partner with faith-based organizations. The faith-based organizations, however, may have the goal of facilitating a transforming belief in God, sure that their goal is the best way to meet the shared objective of reducing out-of-wedlock births. This raises a fundamental policy issue: To what extent can the partnership proceed and on what terms? Faith leaders, acting on principle, may be unable to achieve compromise with government. Even when agreeing on a goal, the faith and government sectors may strongly disagree on the appropriate social action to be taken. Explains Washington, D.C., Mayor Anthony Williams:

> The faith community is obviously—and I don't mean this facetiously— answering to a higher authority. You're not dealing in relative terms, you're dealing in absolute terms: There is good and evil, there is right and wrong. From a kind of theological or principled or moral point of view, what is an acceptable amount of poverty or homelessness? None. I mean zero. So by that definition, every agreement that you may strike is always begrudging, it is always going to be temporary, and it is always going to be challenged later.

Goal incongruence also occurs when government activates a network but also competes against parts of the network. For example, Indianapolis attempted to replace its monopolistic, money-losing public transportation system with a more responsive networked group of for-profit, nonprofit, and government providers of more varied services. As a political compromise, the city kept the position of mobility, or contract, manager inside the existing public transit corporation that ran large city buses. Unfortunately the corporation did not want to lose any business, even if alternative forms of transportation would benefit more riders. This led to tension among network participants. The quasi-public agency running the existing large bus routes, minority-owned companies running feeder routes, and community development corporations transporting urban residents and disabled patrons all operated with different, often competing purposes as the demand for subsidized services exceeded existing revenues.

A third form of goal incongruence can result from the inevitable tension of network members attempting to maximize their own interests, while government pushes its partners to sublimate their interests to the public good. In its worst manifestation, this can result in corruption as a private player improperly uses a government franchise for its own narrow interests. While unfortunate, such unlawful acts can be fairly easily addressed through the legal process. The tougher issue is how to handle genuine, aboveboard differences. Explains Harvard University professor Mark Moore:

It is one thing to say that there is a well-understood, collectively established public purpose which is being usefully pursued through an arrangement in which the purposes remain constant, and only the means of achieving them change; and quite a different thing to say that there are no public purposes other than turning a collectively owned asset over to a partner group to use as it wishes. The issue of how a public purpose is formed and used to discipline and guide the operations of the network, or, somewhat more narrowly, how different partnership arrangements can be evaluated from the point of view of whether the government got enough of what it wanted out of the deal, is constantly important.[2]

Goal congruence, in all three senses of the issue, is a vital and ongoing component of a successful relationship.

Contorted Oversight

Many governments mistakenly see public-private partnerships and outsourcing as a way to offload the headaches of managing a service and fail to exercise adequate oversight. The inevitable result: cost overruns, service failures, and even scandal. New Jersey's Department of Motor Vehicles, for example, has endured several high-profile contracting problems in recent years that were blamed on failed oversight. The cost of these scandals has been high. In 1985 dozens of privately run Department of Motor Vehicles district offices were returned to state control after an audit by the State Commission of Investigation (SCI) discovered lax security, substandard auditing procedures, and inadequate state monitoring of private contractors. Seventeen years later, investigations by the SCI and the state attorney general's office found that state officials had failed to monitor properly the state's troubled privatized emissions inspection system. Both cases stemmed from a breakdown in oversight.

Conversely, public officials may overuse their authority, insisting that providers perform every detail in the contract whether or not it is productive. Often the authority to supervise outputs or outcomes results in government contract monitors intruding on the very processes of networked partners. This intrusion may appear as licensing, code enforcement, questioning the appropriateness of provider techniques, or a host of other mechanisms the state can use to make life difficult for private and non-profit firms.

These two extremes often yield wild pendulum swings: Government, first failing to exercise sufficient oversight, then overreacts when a problem surfaces and attempts to micromanage its partners. When such excessive red tape is imposed on partners, it is most frequently the residue of previous scandals and errors. Milwaukee welfare providers experienced just such a reaction after the media published negative stories about two of the welfare-to-work contractors. Rather than addressing allegations with the specific contractors involved, the state levied additional reporting requirements on all network partners. The system was subsequently overwhelmed by excessive compliance burdens. "We swung the pendulum too far," admits a senior official from the Division of Workforce Solutions. "We put in too many standards, too many data requirements, some of which were more about process than results." Good oversight concentrates on outcomes, not processes.

Communication Meltdown

When a service is provided in-house, informal communication channels within the organization augment formal communication efforts and information flow. These internal "water-cooler" communication channels often suffer under a networked approach, where diffusion and decentralization can create communication difficulties.[3] Moreover, government sometimes imposes unnecessary confidentiality restrictions—not imposed on itself—on its contractors, further disrupting the flow of information. Additionally, when partners use separate, incompatible information systems, the result is uneven communication and poor collaboration. The loss of constant, current, informal communication channels means that sometimes it takes longer to catch problems and react to crises.

Communication problems are not limited to government-initiated networks. The private sector spent billions of dollars during the 1990s in efforts to eliminate this problem, but communication breakdowns between suppliers and producers occur regularly. The Gartner Group lists communication problems as the primary reason that half of all IT (information technology) outsourcing projects fail to deliver on bottom-line promises.[4] For example, communication difficulties resulted in Cisco Systems' $2.2 billion inventory write-down in 2001. In the late 1990s Cisco ramped up its virtual supply chain in response to skyrocketing demands during the Internet and telecommunications boom but then failed to turn it off at the onset of the 2000 technology bust. As a result, Cisco was saddled with a huge inventory of components that no one wanted to buy. Several factors contributed to Cisco's monumental blunder, but the most important was poor communication throughout its supply-chain network. The word that reduced product demand should slow or stop production did not flow quickly enough from company headquarters to the component subcontractors at the middle and bottom of the supply-chain pyramid.[5]

As we illustrate in chapter five, technology can play an important role in solving these communication problems. Knowledge management software, teleconferencing, video conferencing, and remote and electronic managing capabilities all can enhance the process of networking.

However, outdated information technology can also impede better communication. During the anthrax crisis in Washington, D.C., in fall 2001, for example, the Kaiser Permanente health group of the mid-Atlantic states sent its physicians e-mail and phone messages twice a day detailing new guidelines for anthrax treatments. The company also ran an electronic search of patient records to identify hundreds of postal workers who might be at risk of infection, and it contacted them to suggest possible treatments.[6] When Kaiser communicated with the federal government, however, it had to resort to far less sophisticated information-sharing strategies—fax, telephone, and postal mail—because government IT systems were not set up to interact with external partners and many government records were not digitized.

Fragmented Coordination

Networked government typically involves coordination between multiple levels of government, nonprofit organizations, and for-profit companies. Each has its own constituencies, and when complexity is high and responsibility unclear, coordination problems can undermine the network. Poor performance by any one organization—or the breakdown of the relationships between any two organizations—can imperil the performance of the whole.

This risk means that in addition to managing its relationships with each provider, government must also manage relationships among organizations within the network.[7] A mental health network, for example, might consist of an inpatient psychiatric facility, a suicide prevention hotline, a crisis facility, several group housing operators, and a vocational training provider.[8] Not only must the network manager coordinate these entities, but she must also ensure that each provider share information, refer clients to other network providers, and coordinate services. Few government agencies—or nonprofit organizations, for that matter—have figured out how to do this well.

In fact, some government programs may appear to be a networked form of provision, but they so utterly lack coordination that they strain the very definition of a network. One example is the provision of govern-

The Tension between Competition and Collaboration

Achieving both goal congruence and partner collaboration is often complicated by the reality that providers who collaborate in one network must also compete vigorously against each other for contracts and funds elsewhere. This external tension causes underlying tension within the network relationship, which sometimes surfaces as mistrust and information hoarding.

When the U.S. Department of Education evaluated proposals for its large direct-loan processing contract, it short-listed two responses. One was a network solution, integrated by a single vendor. In the other, a single entity provided all the services. The networked solution promised broad reach, with very large companies each bringing specialized capacities into a supposedly seamless solution. But before the department awarded the contract for the networked solution, it carefully probed the network integrator about whether it could, in fact, smoothly manage a team in which the two largest partners were key competitors in many other areas.

We address ways to resolve competitor tensions later in the book, but for now we suggest looking for answers in the private sector. What was unheard of fifteen years ago—competitors collaborating on one project and competing on the next one—is now routine business practice.

ment health services for the elderly who qualify for both Medicare and Medicaid. This high-risk group—dubbed "dual eligibles" by health policy experts—received much attention in the 2003 congressional debate over Medicare prescription drug benefits. The medical needs of dual eligibles, many of whom live in nursing homes, are covered by the federal Medicare program, but state-administered Medicaid programs pay for their drugs. Health care provision for dual eligibles is a sprawling, complex network. In addition to the federal Medicare program and state Medicaid coverage, the "network" involves local agencies, doctors, nursing homes, other care-givers, and private benefit management companies that administer many state drug benefit programs.

In a well-coordinated network—one in which service to individuals is the focal point—the total cost and quality of patient care would be central. Unfortunately, health services for dual eligibles are structured differently. Care and funding is so fragmented that drug decisions are not coordinated with other health care services, and opportunities for "big-picture" care management are lost or nonexistent. Thus, one provider may decide not to use an expensive drug without appreciating that its use would likely reduce subsequent hospitalizations or surgeries.

Data Deficits and Bad Benchmarks

The dearth of accurate data may cause networked service delivery to fail just as it does more straightforward outsourcing. An official considering a network innovation must first determine whether the work should be done through existing hierarchical government networks. The official can make this decision, however, only if he knows the true cost and perfor-mance of the government option. And, usually, he does not. Since gov-ernment has no competition and therefore little incentive to "work lean," it has no need to develop accurate data on exact costs of services. The drivers for developing such data within government are often political, a situation that colors how the data are expressed. How much does it really cost to fill a pothole or process a tax return? Most of the time government itself cannot account for the true costs. "I can't recall doing very many outsourcings where the incumbent in-house provider knew at the outset what its fully loaded costs were to provide a service. In some cases, there was greater clarity around performance measures—but even those were not clear in all areas," says Skip Stitt, who, first as deputy mayor of Indianapolis and then as a private consultant, has worked with dozens of government entities to implement networked approaches. "Moreover," he explains, "even if they did have the data, they might have strong incentives not to share it completely. For example, when a sheriff faces possible outsourcing of the jail to a private company, he has an incentive to understate indirect or even sunk costs. But when he seeks reimbursement for housing prisoners from another jurisdiction, he may have a strong incentive to document and include all costs, no matter how indirect they may be."

The state of Kansas experienced the consequences of data deficits when, in the mid-1990s, it contracted out all foster care, adoption, and family preservation programs. The cost data it gave to the bidders grossly understated the state's true costs. "The problem for us in setting the outcomes was that there [were] no data," explains Teresa Markowitz, former commissioner for children and family services for the state of Kansas. "We had to pull the data out of the air." Not surprisingly, the bids that the state received substantially underpriced the true cost of the services. Subsequently, nearly all providers experienced huge cost overruns in the first two years of the contract. Two providers, both reputable, stable nonprofit organizations, were forced to declare bankruptcy as a result.

Such data failures also create ongoing problems because government officials tend to develop "upward leaping expectations" after contracting a service to external partners. The best becomes an enemy of the better, fostering unrealistic expectations and creating tension among partners. Government must remember where it started and measure success against the original baseline.

Capacity Shortages

In chapter one we briefly addressed the assertion that government has been "hollowed out" because it relies increasingly on contractors to do its business. According to this argument, government has reached the point where it lacks sufficient internal expertise to manage even its contractors.[9] Although there may be some scattered truth to this charge, the overall problem is less the lack of public employees to manage contractors and more the lack of public employees with the right skills or training necessary to effectively manage networks.

Managing network government requires a *different kind of internal capacity* than managing public employees. Good network procurement capacity requires the participation of individuals with broad experience and the ability to see how varied configurations produce different outcomes and how different partners produce differing results. Unfortunately these skills and competencies are in short supply in most governments. The federal government, for example, faces a huge shortage of highly trained project managers to oversee its thousands of multimillion-dollar projects—the majority of which are delivered through various kinds of contracts.

What causes this management shortage? In the United States one culprit is the civil service system. As we discuss in chapter seven, narrow civil service careers unnecessarily restrict talented public employees. Civil service systems developed to help government itself provide services.[10] Under this system, government hires specialists in certain areas. As these employees gain experience in their jobs and become technical experts, they are promoted to manager or supervisor positions. In contrast to most private companies, the civil service system has no real, discernible path for career advancement for those who are simply good project managers or negotiators. "The problem is there is no career path," explains Ana Gallagher, a project manager for the U.S. Department of Agriculture. "If I want to move up in government, I have to leave project management and take over managing an IT department. I don't want to do that."[11]

Two other factors contributing to the management shortage in some agencies are reductions in the number of employees trained in acquisitions and the failure to train existing procurement employees to carry out their jobs effectively in an increasingly complex environment. These problems will intensify as experienced staff retire or leave. About 40 percent of federal acquisitions or procurement officers will be eligible to retire over the next five years.[12]

The growing lack of sophisticated contracting skills in the public sector can be somewhat mitigated by seeking assistance from outside experts in managing large, complex outsourcings. Nevertheless, government must both maintain a core procurement competency and, as the more knowledgeable public officials know, also seek outside acquisition help.

Relationship Stability

Government has the advantage of stability. Over time, public sector service delivery and even its simple bilateral relationships tend to become stable. Partners know what to expect, and even after a contract expires the service may change little. Senior officials and media coverage almost always reward this stable and continued—but often mediocre—effort more than they do the high standards of innovators and the inherent risk they face. Beneficiaries of the status quo, whether they are vendors or clients, also feel threatened by change. In Indianapolis, for example, residents in neglected neighborhoods were comforted by the long-standing presence of community centers funded by the government and United Way, even though many centers provided little actual help and performed erratically. When the city announced that continued funding depended on the centers meeting certain performance standards regarding job placements, the residents protested. Change was not their only concern; their worries also rested on a well-founded skepticism that when city hall said "change" in discussing as the poorest neighborhoods, it really meant cutbacks.

Innovators face the challenge of rewarding high standards and risk taking while working to maintain stable services. When a network is proposed, especially one in which government contracts network management to a third party, concerns are often raised regarding what will happen when the contract expires. This uncertainty fosters aversion to risk taking and wariness among partners about one another. Moreover, if the benefit of the new network is flexibility and performance, then the government contract manager may indeed exercise the right to terminate or substantially alter the contract, thus aggravating anxieties regarding relationship stability.

Procurement officials face the additional challenge of designing into contracts transition plans that provide government enough practical authority to allow it actually to exercise its termination or noncontinuation management rights. These transition provisions may include plans for future ownership of buildings and other capital investments, some control over communication with clients, and participation in other outreach efforts during the contract. Determining in advance how to handle barriers to entry and customer handoffs can dramatically enhance the leverage of contract monitors later.

Improving the Odds

By methodically laying out the benefits and challenges of government by network, we hope to accomplish two things. The first is to help government officials size up and exploit the situations in which a networked approach would be appropriate—and determine when it would not. As illustrated in table 3-1, certain conditions favor a networked model of delivery; certain others support a more traditional hierarchical approach. By evaluating opportunities against these criteria (which are closely related to the advantages and challenges of networked government), policymakers can avoid trying to force a square peg into a round hole.

Second, we want to make it entirely clear that despite the unparalleled opportunities government officials have to improve service quality and cost effectiveness through the use of networks, ample risks and challenges accompany this approach. Addressing these challenges and maximizing the benefits require governments to operate in a new way. Innovative officials

TABLE 3-1   Factors Determining Government's Choice of a Governance Model

Factors favoring network model	Factors favoring hierarchical model
Need for flexibility	Stability preferred
Need for differentiated response to clients or customers	Need for uniform, rule-driven, response
Need for diverse skills	Only a single professional skill needed
Many potential private players available	Government predominant provider
Desired outcome or outputs clear	Outcome ambiguous
Private sector fills skill gap	Government has necessary experience
Leveraging private assets critical	Outside capacity not important
Partners have greater reach or credibility	Government experienced with citizens in this area
Multiple services touch same customer	Service is relatively stand-alone
Third parties can deliver service or achieve goal at lower cost than government	In-house delivery more economical
Rapidly changing technology	Service not affected by changing technology
Multiple levels of government provide service	Single level of government provides service
Multiple agencies use or need similar functions	Single agency uses or needs similar functions

who explicitly understand and address these challenges can mitigate—albeit not eliminate—the problems and increase chances for success.

Part two of this book examines what this new approach entails and how to implement it.

CHAPTER 3—THE BOTTOM LINE

KEY POINTS

▲ Poor performance by any one organization—or the breakdown of the relationships between any two organizations within the network—can imperil the performance of the whole.

▲ Successful network management requires grappling with skill-set, technology, information asymmetry, and cultural issues. The network manager must master the challenges of governing by network: aligning goals, providing oversight, averting communications meltdown, coordinating multiple partners, managing the tension between competition and collaboration, and overcoming data deficits and capacity shortages.

PITFALLS

▲ Failing to exercise sufficient oversight and then responding to problems by overreacting and attempting to micromanage the partners.

▲ Failing to align goals among the network partners.

▲ Forming a network containing competitors as partners without analyzing their compatibility.

TIPS

▲ Refrain from overwhelming network partners with excessive compliance burdens.

▲ Benchmark cost and quality before asking for bids.

▲ Fashion transition plans that allow government to retain enough practical authority to enable it to actually exercise its termination rights.

EXAMPLES

▲ *Milwaukee Welfare to Work.* Composed almost wholly of nongovernmental organizations, Milwaukee's integrated welfare-to-work service delivery system is one of the country's most sophisticated social service networks. The Milwaukee experience illustrates both the tremendous promise and the myriad complexities of government by network.

▲ *New Jersey Department of Motor Vehicles.* The agency has endured several high-profile contracting problems in recent years. Critics target inadequate oversight as the main reason for New Jersey's difficulties.

PART 2

Managing by Network

FOUR

Designing the Network

When you put out a bid for a network, you're usually building a network that doesn't currently exist, which means you need to think on a broader basis than linearly. Doing this right requires a conceptual feel for how it should turn out in the end.

—John Koskinen, former city administrator, Washington, D.C.

A network that delivers effective public services doesn't just happen. Someone must first figure out how to fuse a collection of private and public organizations into a seamless service delivery system. The job of this network designer is to identify possible partners, bring all the relevant stakeholders to the table, analyze the current in-house operations, determine and communicate to all members the expectations of how the network will function, assemble and enmesh the pieces of the network, devise strategies to maintain the network, and, finally, activate it.[1] The designer faces the challenge of creating a model malleable enough to accommodate each partner, dynamic enough to adjust to changing circumstances, but fixed enough in mission to serve the common goal.

The success or failure of a networked approach can often be traced to the original design. Network governance structures the flow of information and resources within the network. Like a good road map, a sound design

55

helps government reach its ultimate policy and operational destination. Even slight design flaws can generate considerable problems later on, wasting partners' time and energy—no matter how well the network is managed. Governments can avoid these problems by using the design phase to address upfront many of the toughest issues involved in formulating and managing networks.

In particular, the design phase entails answering five major questions:

▲ What goals does the government hope to accomplish?
▲ Which tools will be used to form and activate the network?
▲ Who are the most appropriate partners to help government accomplish its goals?
▲ How should the network be designed given the professed goals?
▲ How should the network be governed and managed?

Mission and Strategy: Answering the "What" Question

All too often, precious little thought is given to the questions of mission and strategy: what are the policy goals the agency hopes to fulfill, and how do these goals dictate what the members of the network should do. Instead, agency officials pick up their organizational chart, find something they are not doing very well, and then ask the private sector to do it for them, never questioning whether that narrow task furthers its mission. In this way networked government sometimes fails, not because of how a particular venture is managed, but because of what was delegated to the network in the first place. By starting first with mission and then configuring the process, network government can offer a fundamental change from traditional government that often looks first to process and then to mission.

The government executive, hamstrung by precedent and constrained by well-intentioned bureaucratic practices, will often find it very difficult to step into the larger, more important, and more exciting role of conceptualizing the new models and solutions critical to the success of networked government. The destination, not the path, should be the organizing theme around which the components and interactions of the network are built.

When school officials at the Montaigne secondary school near The Hague in the Netherlands needed additional school capacity, for example, they could have chosen the usual route of getting bids to build a school from several contractors. They concluded, however, that what they really wanted to buy was not simply a physical asset—in this case a school building—but instead a quality learning environment produced by such services as cleaning, caretaking, security, grounds maintenance, information technology, and so on. It was not the product—the school building—that was key, but the services, as well as the availability of the school building. School teachers and officials now spend all their time on the core mission, teaching children, while a consortium of private firms handles everything else. Dozens of school authorities in the United Kingdom have also adopted this innovative output-oriented model.

Ask the Right Question

As the Netherlands school example demonstrates, formulating the right strategy means, first of all, focusing on the core mission of the organization and asking the pivotal question: What outcome-based public value is the agency trying to create?

Answering this question forces government officials to determine their policy goals and the exact role their agency should play in fulfilling those goals. For example, a housing authority administrator facing a lack of affordable housing might ask, "Is my job to build housing units, or to maximize the number of people who can own and occupy their own homes?" If the answer is the latter, then the central task may not be to construct public housing, by contract or otherwise. Instead, the task might

---

Key Principles for Determining Government's Goals

✔ Determine the important public value
✔ Do not define the problem or the answer through the narrow lens of historical processes
✔ Calibrate the design of the network to the desired outcome

be to convene, seed, and direct the necessary resources that will help the agency expand homeownership.

This thought process guided Washington mayor Anthony Williams and his staff as they conducted a top-to-bottom review of the city's health system soon after Williams took office in the late 1990s. For nearly two centuries D.C. General Hospital had been the backbone of the district's public health system. In recent years, however, the city-owned hospital, plagued by poor management, hemorrhaged cash. Instead of asking, "How can we fix the hospital?" Williams asked a more fundamental question: "Is it my job to run a public hospital or to provide the maximum public health for the indigent?" Recalls former city administrator John Koskinen: "The District [of Columbia] had some of the worst health statistics in the country. The discussion was less about whether or not we should be running a hospital, and more about how to improve these statistics. We took a step back and asked: What is the action that will improve health care in the city the most?"

Framed this way, the answer was obvious. Close D.C. General and instead use the city subsidy for the hospital to knit together a network of private hospitals and community-based health clinics. District officials believed that this approach would not only save taxpayers money but also produce higher-quality health care for more people. "We decided that government should maybe not be in the business of running hospitals, and instead we should be providing health care to those who need it," says Koskinen. "We now have a better health care safety net for the city's indigent than we were able to provide before at D.C. General."

Forming the D.C. health care network enabled Mayor Williams to do something else: unlock the underutilized capacity of the myriad clinics and private hospitals located throughout the city. By linking the health networks together using public dollars, he could create greater overall value than when the clinics operated in isolation from other providers. In this way, the association among the providers empowered them all and energized the city's overall health care system. The network did experience some bumps along the road—largely caused by the bankruptcy of one of the key health care providers—but even so, the system managed to provide far more choices, at a lower overall cost, than the city had offered when it concentrated its attention and resources in one place.

Step Outside the Box

A government agency should not let its historical processes, current organizational charts, existing capabilities, or, for that matter, the private sector's current offerings dictate the activities that should transition to a networked approach. When outsourcing occurs in a procurement box inside a narrowly conceived functional channel based mostly on processes that are not working well, costs can go down and quality up, but often the benefit is artificially constrained. When the process is the problem, changing the components does not help much. In contrast, using a networked model as a lever creates new solutions and transforms existing operations. Explains Stan Soloway, president of the Professional Services Council, based in Washington, D.C.:

> In the private sector there's the notion of "design space," which refers to the space needed to design to an outcome, rather than a preconceived notion of what it should look like. When I was at DoD [Department of Defense], we spent a day at Federal Express. The key point hammered into us was that the key to success is recognizing that before you outsource, you need to completely reassess everything you're doing today, do a process map, and then get rid of anything you're now doing that doesn't plug into your new model.

This is the approach adopted by the U.S. Coast Guard when it sought to modernize its deepwater fleet. It completely rethought its strategy for purchasing goods and services when it requested bids for fleet modernization. The old, $10 billion fleet, which consisted of 90 ships and 200 aircraft, was falling apart and unsuited to present-day conditions. The standard way of replacing it would have been to purchase each plane, boat, and piece of technology separately as they wore out and only later figure out how to put them all together. The Coast Guard opted for a much different model: contracting with one consortium to replace its entire inventory as an integrated package over a multiyear time frame. The agency challenged bidders in its request for proposal (RFP) to show how they would increase mission effectiveness and streamline operations through the use of better and newer technologies. The RFP spelled out what outcomes the agency hoped to achieve and what capabilities it needed—search and rescue, detecting someone adrift in the ocean, providing surge capacity to meet national security, and meeting disaster-response requirements—and then left it to the vendors (with help from teams of Coast Guard specialists assigned to the three final bidders) to design the system of boats, ships, aircraft, satellites, information technology, and unmanned aerial vehicles that was needed. The ultimate goal: to transform the way the Coast Guard does its job.

Initiation Strategies

Governing by network is neither an excuse for, nor as simple as, privatization, because it recognizes that in a highly complex society a variety of people and organizations will be necessary to provide high-quality citizen services. The quality in large part derives from the learning that occurs at diverse points in the network. Therefore as a mayor, department head, or entrepreneurial manager looks to make a difference, the threshold question should not be how do I issue a request for proposal to the private sector or direct the people who work for me to do more, but rather how do I bring together the resources necessary to execute my mission as well as possible. Creative officials possess a variety of assets they can deploy to initiate a progressive response.

Money

In some ways money is both the simplest and, at times, least effective way to forge the relationships that produce true value. The power of government to dole out money, through a grant or contract, obviously can procure the attention of other potential participants. Money spent through traditional procurement vehicles, however, often solicits narrow and unimaginative responses. Of course creative government managers can broadly structure a request in a way that encourages myriad groups to form a network, but this sweeping, open-ended process (discussed later in the book) is still fairly unusual.

Rhetoric

Ideas and rhetoric can unite partners as well. Elected officials can use the bully pulpit to convene organizations around an important idea. President

George W. Bush's speech in Los Angeles in March 2004, for example, drew thousands of people who wanted to hear how they could partner with their communities generally and, more specifically, how they could help the 600,000 inmates that would be released from prison that year.

Mayor Bill Purcell of Nashville articulated his goal to produce 100,000 new or rehabilitated units of affordable housing and, to this end, brought together pastors, builders, several community development corporations, and city planners. The product, of course, often involves more than simply hammers and nails. As Mayor Purcell explains, "There is a recruitment of resources in construction, but there is also an engagement or involvement in the recruitment of people to live in the house, the support of the family in the neighborhood during the critical early days of ownership, occupancy, and citizenship."

Appointed officials can also pull together groups around important public matters. For example, a respected parks director might articulate the vision that every child in the city will live within a half mile of green space and linear parks. Around this message the parks director can convene schools, waterway and trail advocates, private recreational groups like the YMCA, and others to discuss strategies for achieving the goal.

Similarly, an issue such as reducing teen pregnancy can be the organizing theme, whether asserted by the elected official or the public health official. The nature of the issue thus often defines the communities from which the network will form. Campaigns against teen pregnancy can unify a network of school, parent, faith, medical, and community organizations whose differing approaches to a common issue of interest can attack that issue from all sides, solving problems and benefiting the broader community through a concerted approach. Thus how the pieces connect—that is, their network—multiplies their individual effectiveness.

Capacity to Convene

A public official can also bring together parties whose deep yet narrow knowledge will provoke valuable discoveries when deployed in conjunction with others. Often nonprofit organizations are so overwhelmed with demands for their core services that they lack the time or the resources to find and interact with others even in the same sphere. Using her convening authority as a catalyst, an official can provide a venue for organizations and individuals with similar goals to meet, discover common ground, and perhaps even find ways of dividing labor and sharing resources, making each more effective and efficient than before.

Several years ago, Graham Richard, the Mayor of Fort Wayne, Indiana, noticed too many disconnected pieces in a particular underserved neighborhood. He saw that the neighborhood wanted a new library and needed new locations for its after-school (run by the Urban League) and Head Start programs. He observed needs and resources isolated from each other. Mayor Richard invited the relevant players to his office, including representatives from the prominent Catholic and Lutheran churches in the neighborhood. "By using the convening authority," he explained, "and by tapping the commitment of Catholic and Lutheran organizations that owned important parcels of land . . . we created a new initiative, which is a campus with a library, an after-school program, a Head Start Program, and the Urban League headquarters." Richard thus leveraged the city's land use authority with the important role of convening: "Convening authority is one of the most important assets that a mayor has in a community—just getting people to come in a room who have never met each other or talked to each other because they're in their silos of service. . . . and all of a sudden they start saying, 'Well, I didn't know you were doing that. . . . What if we started to work together.' "

People and Technology Resources

A public official can also add resources, in the form of people or technology, to help activate a network. In Indianapolis, the Front Porch Alliance, an initiative that brought together hundreds of faith-based and community organizations in cooperative projects, succeeded. How? A handful of people assigned to the mayor's office did nothing more than go door-to-door in selected neighborhoods linking dedicated citizens and organizations, fostering their collaboration by finding information and people who could help them, and then clearing away any barriers. These city employees provided the much-needed infrastructure upon which a group of previously unrelated residents and groups began to interact.

Government officials can provide the tools for networks to succeed in other ways. Often government possesses, or is willing to purchase, relatively inexpensive technology that can integrate data from various computer systems, allowing organizations to cooperate that otherwise would be walled off from each other. Florida recently announced a technology initiative to improve and integrate the data of diverse organizations that provide services to children by helping them share information in real time. The state will pay for handheld wireless tools, mainframe integration, and software that can be deployed throughout the private, nonprofit, and public entities that make up the state's decentralized child welfare system.

Absent the state's intervention, child welfare would have remained more of a group of unrelated services rather than a tightly integrated network. In most cities, child welfare workers, school social workers, juvenile court probation officers, police juvenile workers, and child-serving community organizations typically do not share information about a troubled child, let alone information about other problematic siblings or parents. As a result, the many points of interaction, each of which could produce a valuable insight, rarely are gathered together to produce the knowledge necessary to help the child. By providing the infrastructure for better communications among these many providers, Florida hopes to form a more structured child welfare network that increases coordinated decisionmaking.

Authority

Government can also use its authority more explicitly as a resource to form a network. For example, a presiding judge can use her authority to bring together a range of providers to develop a more effective method for dealing with a specific problem or population, such as drug users. The selected "loaned" use of judicial authority to participating organizations not only gives the organizations leverage over the offenders but also produces better solutions and more learning as the organizations previously acting independently share knowledge and often "clients" as an individual makes progress.

James Payne, the juvenile court judge in Marion County, Indiana, used this approach when the county faced a crisis of inadequate services for troubled children. The ad hoc groups involved in providing services to the children, many of them wards of the court, did not collectively offer what the judge believed was the right mix of help. He dramatically improved the system when he brought new providers and faith-based groups together and combined them with an organization trained in intake and diagnostic work. Thus official authority created a network of integrated services that produced more services and shared information to power better decisions.

Authority can be "loaned" in a variety of ways. For instance, in many cities the process of certifying a community development corporation carries with it advantages in terms of neighborhood authority and federal funding. Formal recognition of a group by city hall confers a tangible value. When police departments designate neighborhood advisory councils or official crime watch groups, their authority brings a status to those groups that can generate new points of interaction and enhanced services.

Choosing the Right Partners

As University of Vermont professor Phillip Cooper has observed, "the entire network is only as strong as its weakest component," which makes choosing each partner critical, especially in a network designed to deliver a particular service or product.[2] Searching for the best potential partners is a matter of determining which assets provided by other players could work most effectively for the government. The question is which actors in which ways when brought together can produce more positive results per dollar and unit of effort than government alone. The person responsible for answering this question must be able to separate the mission into components and concurrently begin mining new assets.

The factors that will be the most important in choosing the right partners—and the weight assigned to each factor—will change depending on the particular circumstances. For example, if the purpose of the network is to strengthen a community, then government officials will look to partners within the community. If the purpose is delivery of a technical service, then the scan will include quality technology providers. If the network's mission demands a well-defined value, such as reducing teen pregnancy through abstinence, then the partners should share that value. A few broad criteria, however, can help governments distinguish the most appropriate partners.

Cultural Compatibility

To ensure a long-standing, mutually beneficial relationship, selecting network partners requires attention to cultural compatibility. The cultural issues will vary depending on the nature of the network. For example, if the purpose of the network is to implement a new policy—as in the work-first approach in welfare-to-work networks—then the partner organizations and their involved officials need to share that value. Indeed in this situation government policymakers turned to a network approach to facilitate or procure cultural change from others that they could not produce in their own bureaucracies.

In contrast, if the purpose is more in the nature of a supply chain, then the issues that must be aligned have more to do with price, quality, timeliness, and any trade-offs among these factors. In these cases, technical issues can become mission issues. Take a call center operation. What is more important? Answering as many questions as possible during that first call? Answering and disposing of calls quickly? Or saving money by driving citizens to e-government services? If these kinds of issues are not explicitly dealt with in choosing partners, then the divergent beliefs around these issues can eventually become value chasms that endanger the relationship.

Operational Capacity

Operational excellence provides the most straightforward and common prism through which to evaluate potential partners. In these cases, the government entity seeks technology, experience, and skills. For example, when the federal Department of Education decided to rebuild its outdated student loan system, it reviewed the market to identify which potential partners could both integrate existing functions and build and operate a new system. The subsequent request for proposal caused several competitors to join forces to form a consortium that brought the department technology it could never have built or afforded itself. Observing the need for collaboration, these private sector forces joined to fulfill the need without the command and control mechanisms government entities often require to forge cooperation.

In evaluating the operational capacity of potential partners, several factors are typically important:

Cost. Can the network partner perform the activity for less money than it costs currently? Although cost should almost never be the sole—nor even the main—consideration when outsourcing to a network, it is an important factor whenever taxpayer dollars are being spent.

Specialized expertise. Often one of the principal reasons for using a networked model is to help the public sector gain the specialized expertise of "best-in-class" providers. Companies with managers that wake up every day brainstorming better and quicker ways to tow cars will, more often than not, be better at this task than any city manager with dozens of other operational responsibilities. Similarly, a company with national or worldwide scale in a particular area can hone skills at a level impossible for government by sharing best practices and innovations across cities, states, and even countries.

Financial viability. Partners should be stable enough financially to weather storms of market volatility and survive the loss of individual con-

Wisconsin Family Partnership Initiative

One form of specialized expertise that government might seek out is the ability to integrate a network. Fourteen Wisconsin counties joined together to create the Family Partnership Initiative because they wanted to provide intensive case management that would allow children to be treated across a range of integrated services. Wisconsin formed a multicounty system out of a group of discrete pieces, but none of the counties had the requisite skills at the scale necessary to integrate the network. A search of area assets helped the multicounty partnership identify an organization, Lutheran Family Services, which had the needed integration skills and experience.

tracts. Financial viability is a particularly important criterion for prime contractors.

Ability to assume some risk. Not all the partners in a network need to assume risk, but at least some of them, particularly the integrator, should be capable of assuming performance and financial risks over which it has control.

Proximity to the Customer

In some instances the government is looking for a way to communicate effectively with a particular population. The population might be dispersed, in which case an organization with broad reach is required. This was an important reason the White House teamed with business associations as part of the Y2K initiative to ensure that computers could handle the rollover from 1999 to 2000. In other cases the government service is delivered on a small, neighborhood scale, where existing credibility is an issue. In either case the partners are closer to the customer than government.

Neighborhood ties. A government-envisioned program often lacks existing ongoing relationships with customers close to where they live. To rectify this, instead of opening a government office, creative public managers often search for a neighborhood partner with existing access to the community. The neighborhood partner might not even necessarily be in a business similar to what the government proposes; it simply needs to be able to provide access. When Indianapolis outsourced much of its workforce training, the training specialists lacked neighborhood ties in many cases. So they turned to small local and faith-based groups, which served as the front door for a broad array of services delivered by others.

Legitimacy. Sometimes the government's efforts are supported by too little community support, a deficit that needs to be repaired by the network. This is exactly what the New York State Division of Parole did when it recruited a local community group, La Bodega de Familia, as its partner. La Bodega had strong support from the community through its work with families. By partnering with La Bodega, the parole department enhanced its legitimacy and more easily convinced anxious families that

Leveraging Existing Structures and Institutions

Sometimes initiating a networked approach requires that networks be created out of whole cloth, but more often than not, governments will be able to engage existing structures and institutions in forming the network.

When it became apparent that computer programs might not recognize the rollover from 1999 to 2000, President Bill Clinton summoned John Koskinen into the Oval Office and charged him with averting a Y2K meltdown. He could not have conferred a broader charge. Y2K threatened to wreak havoc not only on local, state, and federal government systems, but possibly even more important, on private sector information systems running everything from power grids to Wall Street. System malfunctions could have disastrous consequences for the U.S. economy.

At that moment, standing in the president's office, Koskinen had no idea how he would pull off such a monumental task. But there was one thing he did know: a big, bureaucratic approach would not work. "You can't command and control large organizations," Koskinen explained. "You have to network across lots of areas and build off existing institutions and structures."

So Koskinen kept his staff small. Some members of Congress literally begged him to hire more people, but he politely declined, knowing that even if he had thousands of staff, he still would not have anywhere near enough people to handle such a huge task through a traditional hierarchical governmental approach. Instead of building a bureaucratic empire, Koskinen fulfilled his charge by influencing the thousands of industry and government associations with whom businesses and state and local governments were already interacting on a regular basis. When it became apparent that the local gas stations were moving at a snail's pace in bringing their gas pump payment systems into Y2K compliance, for example, Koskinen did not try to bring the power of the White House to bear. Instead, he sought out the assistance of oil and gas industry association leaders, who promptly suggested that gas deliveries might not be prudent to all stations whose pumps were not Y2K compliant. Problem solved.

Instead of creating more authority—a time-consuming, expensive, and often unpopular undertaking—Koskinen used the system in place to effect change. By drawing from existing relationships and structures of thousands of powerful associations, Koskinen created what *National Journal* writer Sydney Freedberg Jr. has called a network of networks. "We weren't there to tell them what to do or to regulate them into compliance," Koskinen said. "What we wanted was a partnership. We accomplished our goals by developing relationships of trust with all kinds of agencies and companies and associations."

they needed to support parole efforts to keep the offenders from return-
ing to prison.

Determining the Right Type of Network

Determining which type of network best meets a government's needs
requires first exploring the different types of networks available. As a
result of our conversations with practitioners and experts about networks
in government, we identified six different types of networks that governments use. But our list is by no means exhaustive.[3] Its purpose is simply
to demonstrate that network models come in a variety of forms and serve
various purposes.

Service Contract

In service contract networks, governments use contractual arrangements
as organization tools. Contractor and subcontractor service agreements
and relationships create an array of vertical and horizontal connections as
opposed to simple one-to-one relationships. Such networks are prevalent
in many areas of the public sector, including health, mental health, welfare, child welfare, transportation, and defense.

Supply Chain

Supply-chain networks are formed to deliver a complex product to government, such as a fighter jet or multimodal transportation system. Far
fewer supply-chain networks are found in the public sector than in the private sector because government primarily delivers services, as opposed to
manufacturing goods. Supply-chain networks are found mainly in the
defense and transportation segments.

Ad Hoc

Governments often activate a network in response to a specific situation—
usually an emergency. For example, an ad hoc network of hospitals, doctors,
and public health and law enforcement agencies spring up to attempt to
contain an outbreak of an infectious disease or to respond to natural dis-
asters and cyber-threats.

Channel Partnership

Companies and nonprofits conduct transactions on behalf of government agencies in the same way that retail stores act as a distribution channel for manufacturers. When you purchase a new car, for example, the dealership may handle your motor vehicle registration for you. Other examples include purchasing a fishing license at a sporting goods store or using the Intuit or H&R Block website to file your taxes online. The number of channel partnerships will expand as more and more companies bundle public sector transactions into their online services offerings.

Information Dissemination

To disseminate public information, a government entity can partner with nonprofit and for-profit organizations with resources, such as websites, that make information widely available. Government can use information dissemination methods already in place to communicate with the public. Earth 911, for example, provides a wealth of environmental information and real-time data on its website, such as which local businesses recycle used oil filters. It is able to do this by linking a federal agency, fifty state agencies, thousands of local governments, and countless community groups and nonprofit organizations into one nationwide environmental network.

Civic Switchboard

In this instance government uses its broader perspective to connect diverse organizations in a manner in which they augment each other's capacity to produce an important public outcome. Both because of its elected authority to represent all the citizens and because of its broad responsibilities, the public sector brings a unique perspective that can be used to connect civic organizations that provide a service but are in need of resources with others that might have the needed resources. Connecting the players produces new net value. Government might, in a simple case, bring about the formation of a network of food pantries to help shelters take care of the homeless.

FIGURE 4.1 Types of Public-Private Networks

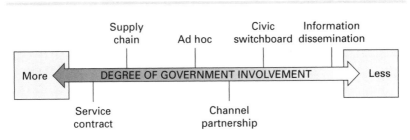

For example, a housing or planning director who wants to increase home ownership might find that a primary reason for lower-than-expected home ownership in a neighborhood is limited access to credit. To solve the credit problem, the director might pull together home ownership counseling and debt consolidation assistance. She might also bring in an intermediary to help those who are distrustful of and inexperienced in communicating with financial organizations. Government's chief contribution in this case is not so much providing money—though that helps—but using the influence and knowledge it has to get the network started, enabling the other sectors to produce the component parts of the solution (figure 4-1).

How to Choose the Right Network

Whether a government uses one of these types of networks or fashions something slightly or radically different, answering the following questions can help public officials figure out what type of network makes the most sense for the particular circumstances:

▲ What do you want to do? Deliver a service? Provide information? Build an aircraft carrier? The overarching purpose is the main determinant in choosing an appropriate network. If the main goal is to increase reach, for example, then government might select a channel partnership, which takes advantage of the private sector's greater reach in the marketplace.

▲ Is the need ongoing or one-time? Does the network only need to be activated in response to a specific event—an emergency or a disaster, for example—or is the need for the network ongoing?

▲ How much money is available? The less money available, the less feasible it will be to create a contractual network, which is typically held together almost exclusively by public dollars.

▲ What is the relative importance of accountability versus flexibility? The more important accountability is as a goal, the more likely it is that a contractual network with clear goals and performance incentives will be the best approach. If flexibility is more important than accountability, then a looser framework may be more appropriate.

The Arizona Motor Vehicles Department (MVD) went through this kind of process in the 1990s. Meteoric population growth in the state placed huge strains on the department's operational capacities (the population increased 30 percent from 1990 to 1998). The growth meant more vehicles, more drivers, more car rentals, more commercial vehicle fleets, and therefore more demand for services provided by the MVD.[4] During the 1990s the MVD's workload was increasing at an annual rate of 13 percent. Meanwhile, state government was carrying out a series of tax reductions and a policy of zero growth in spending and staffing. The combination of the growing population and the spending freeze forced the MVD to search for ways to meet the growing service demand without a corresponding growth in funds or personnel. The result: the MVD's Third Party Program, an initiative to improve customer service, reduce costs, and manage the MVD workload more efficiently by enlisting third-party providers to administer some of the transactions that previously would have been done exclusively by the MVD staff.

While the Third Party Program shifts some of the MVD's work to the private sector, the approach the agency took differed from traditional privatization efforts. The MVD did not want to rely on a drawn-out bidding process or a single contractor to establish an outsourced service structure. Moreover, the agency did not have the budget dollars to be able to pay providers to offer the services on its behalf. Rather than put a service out for bid and award a contract to a single provider, the third-party statute was written to allow any number of third parties to offer services, so long as they were duly qualified and authorized and met compliance standards set by the program. In fact, a key provision of the program was that no single third party could have exclusive rights to a service. This "many provider" aspect of the program was the cornerstone of MVD's competitive government approach to doing business. The third parties also would have to pay for their start-up and ongoing operational costs, thereby relieving MVD of the expense associated with staffing and facilities.

Rather than a traditional service contract network, the MVD created what we call a channel partnership with the private sector. The agency engaged the private sector to offer another channel for Arizona citizens to handle motor vehicle transactions such as vehicle title and registration, driver's license services, and inspections. Using the motivations already in the marketplace, the state of Arizona saved resources by empowering interested parties to provide services normally furnished by government entities, all the while complying with government requirements. All in all, the MVD has partnered with more than seventy outside organizations since the program began in the mid-1990s. One of the best known is ServiceArizona, a partnership with IBM to provide a multichannel electronic service delivery system. Customers can complete their annual vehicle registration renewal on the Internet or by using an interactive voice response system on the telephone. ServiceArizona was the first such electronic delivery system in the country.

The Third Party Program has been successful. Third parties now administer half of the commercial driver's license road tests conducted in the state. These organizations are especially valuable as they typically work for such entities as school districts, government agencies, and private companies with fleets of large vehicles that require the operator to have a commercial license. For example, an authorized third-party examiner for a school district can arrange and administer the driving test to new school bus drivers, saving the district considerable time in bringing new drivers on board.

All in all, the transactions completed through the MVD's network of partners are the equivalent of work done by 200 full-time state employees and represent annual cost avoidance for MVD of more than $6 million in staff, facilities, overhead, and other expenses. Arizona public officials had

Coping with Change: Creating a Flexible Network Design

The structure of government with its lumbering personnel process and its self-inflicted legal constraints limits flexibility. Networking, through alliances with the highly fluid private sector, allows governments to adapt better to changing circumstances. For this reason, an inflexible network violates its very purpose.

As we demonstrated earlier, one reason networks form is to continuously capture the value created through the many points of interchange in the network. This benefit will be lost unless the ability to make frequent changes—and make them quickly—is built into the network design. The network should have the ability to:

▲ Add or subtract partners or services
▲ Broaden or shrink its scope
▲ Incorporate missing elements
▲ Allow and share unanticipated successes
▲ Collaboratively manage unplanned failures
▲ Revise performance goals

A dynamic network continuously identifies new sources of value not explicitly authorized in the original contract and allows for innovation to be quickly deployed. It should also be able to respond to environmental shocks such as contractor bankruptcies, contract problems, or an economic downturn that make it difficult to reach a hoped-for outcome. A flexible structure can help a network cope with this kind of uncertainty by allowing organizations to respond quickly to unforeseen events—for example, by redesigning aspects of the network or adding another partner or two.

Sometimes even getting the network design right may entail an iterative, trial-and-error process. In the early 1990s the city of Indianapolis decided that delivering workforce training services directly should not be the core mission of the Private Industry Council. Instead of producing job training services, the council should be buying them. As a result, the council transformed itself from being a direct service provider to being a contract manager of a network of providers, each of which was paid a fixed fee for every person that it was able to get into a job and off welfare. In time, however, city staff realized that this role was too narrow; people with myriad problems needed a lot of assistance, not just two or three months of help. Compensation systems and the choice of partners both needed adjustment. In response, the city modified the design by expanding the public-private network to include faith-based and community organizations that specialized in helping those with physical or mental disabilities, and it allowed higher rates of compensation for these more difficult cases.

to think outside the box, keep goals rather than processes foremost, and use structures already in place to make it happen.

Who Should Integrate the Network . . . and What Should Be Integrated?

In today's age of specialization and outsourcing, manufacturing an automobile requires managing a large and complex network of suppliers that cumulatively provide the hundreds of individual components that go into assembling the vehicle. Traditionally manufacturers managed these suppliers themselves. Increasingly, however, some automobile companies have begun to divest responsibility for managing large components of the assembly process—such as building the car's interior—to companies that specialize in this process. The same phenomenon is taking place in many other industries from computers to apparel. Behind this trend is the belief that sometimes someone else can better integrate and manage the various processes and organizations that make up the network than can the company itself.

Just as building an automobile requires integrating complex networks of organizations, so too does fulfilling many government responsibilities in today's complex world, whether it is responding to a terrorist threat or coordinating services for someone enrolled in a welfare-to-work program. The intentionally created networks we discuss here require some kind of integrator (in contrast to less formal and less durable formations that often spring up). A strong integrator that can coordinate activities, handle problems, and ensure the provision of quality services is a critical component of a well-designed network.[5] This organizer acts as the "hub" and often is the only entity with links to all the other network participants. As governments rely more and more on networks for delivering services, they face the same fundamental questions as manufacturers: What processes should be integrated, and who should do the integrating?

We take up these questions separately, starting with the latter one: who should do the integrating? Governments have three choices when it comes to determining who should shoulder the difficult task of integrating the network: They can be their own integrator and manage the day-to-day operations of the network in-house; they can delegate all the integration tasks to the prime contractor; or they can hire a third party to coordinate the network.

Government as Integrator

Government has a long history and tradition in serving as its own integrator of large, complex public-private networks ranging from the Manhattan Project during World War II to the more recent Ohio Department of Motor Vehicles' network of more than 200 private motor vehicle office franchises. In many respects the public sector represents a logical choice as the administrator and integrator of the network. A public agency can use its positional authority and perceived impartiality to bring the different parties together, coordinate their activities, and resolve any disputes (figure 4-2).

Yet government also faces some real challenges in being its own integrator. Procurement laws often restrict the ability of public officials to negotiate with potential members of a network on any basis other than simple price considerations.[6] Moreover, government may need to enlist specialized talents to evaluate which partners should be included in the network, a skill that many government officials do not have because of their limited breadth of experience in such matters.

The HOPE VI housing initiative demonstrates how difficult—though not impossible—it can be for government to be its own integrator. The Department of Housing and Urban Development (HUD) introduced the program in 1992 with the goal of reversing decades of public housing failures. HOPE VI promised something for every constituency. To residents it promised new and better housing without displacement. To abutting neighbors it promised to tear down the concentrated blight of public housing and build something less dense, nicer, and more in keeping with the neighborhood. To social service organizations and other localized stakeholders, it promised dollars and participation. And if that were not enough, the initiative accepted the task of moving residents, not just into good housing, but into meaningful work leading to self-sufficiency.

To fulfill the various program goals—ranging from individual self-sufficiency to housing—the HOPE VI networks sought to bring together groups with diverse missions, many of which had never worked together

FIGURE 4.2   Government as Integrator

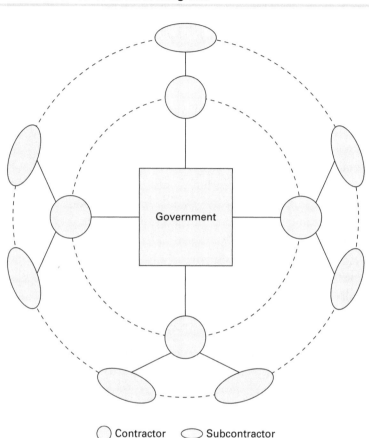

◯ Contractor   ◖ Subcontractor

before. To HUD officials, the logical partners to serve as the integrator of these organizations were the local public housing authorities (PHAs). The experience of the average PHA, however, related primarily to applying complex HUD rules to the management of public housing units. HOPE VI required an entirely different set of skills. PHAs now needed to be knowledgeable about community matters and real estate development and skilled in assembling complex financing structures. They also had to know how to coordinate externally with social service groups to help individuals with multiple problems become self-sufficient.[7]

Some housing authorities—particularly those with very strong executive leadership and city hall backing—proved capable of bringing together the often unruly groups involved in HOPE VI programs and securing the right private talent to integrate the dozens of involved partners. Such was the case in Raleigh, North Carolina, where housing authority director Steve Beam managed to pull together diverse groups to revitalize housing and the surrounding neighborhood. The Halifax Court housing project in downtown Raleigh was demolished, and in its place Beam and his partners constructed Capitol Park, consisting of a one-acre park, a community building, a day-care facility, and six learning centers for youth and adults. The PHA's partners included construction companies and well-respected organizations such as Communities in Schools, the Boys and Girls Clubs, the Junior League, and the Raleigh Hurricanes hockey team.

Yet across the country mismanagement has often marked the HOPE VI program. Squabbles among the partners, high unit costs, confusion over mission, and endless delays—complicated by multiple levels of government all requiring approvals—have added up to create crippling backlogs. Most PHAs simply have not had the necessary skills and expertise to sort out the conflicting missions and be effective integrators of diverse community and construction networks, or to put together complex real estate or multifaceted welfare-to-work programs. Moreover, apart from some initial HOPE VI money, housing directors had few assets with which to hold the network entities together over time.

As a result, some members of Congress have disparaged the program because of its expense, and others have been troubled by the inability of many cities to spend their HOPE VI dollars well—or sometimes even at all. President Bush went even further, recommending that the HOPE VI program be eliminated. The lesson is clear: in certain instances, government can act as its own general contractor. This role, however, requires the government executive to think creatively across service lines and agencies, build an intergovernmental network, and find internal management talent that can creatively configure the best possible solution. Absent this, the government executive must recognize that an outside provider with the skill to integrate the parties properly may, in fact, be the most important asset to procure. A list of criteria to consider in determining whether the government itself should act as integrator is presented in the box.

Prime Contractor as Integrator

Just as it often makes more sense to hire a general contractor to build your home rather than to try and hire—and manage—a slew of contractors yourself, so too it is often in the best interests of a public agency to hire an expert to integrate the network. This was the reasoning behind the Coast Guard's decision to hire Lockheed to manage the modernization of its deepwater fleet. Explains Randy Williamson, the co-author of a General Accounting Office (GAO) report on the deepwater project:

> When contracts have gotten into trouble before, it's usually because the oversight and expertise wasn't there to make it happen. In this case, the Coast Guard didn't have the expertise or the capacity to do this. They would have needed over 1,000 people to manage the different contractors and subcontractors if they did it in-house. By hiring Lockheed, they were hiring an expert to do it for them.

Governments lacking the in-house capabilities to integrate the network themselves frequently use the Coast Guard's model of contracting for an

---

Should Government Itself Act as Integrator?

1. Do the right skill sets, experience, and resources exist within government to oversee the network? If so, where?
2. Do the right skill sets for overseeing the network exist outside of government ? If so, are they superior to those within government?
3. How much managerial attention can and should government devote internally to managing the network?
4. How close does the government agency need to be to actual service delivery?
5. Which integration model best enhances accountability?
6. How important is start-up speed?
7. Does government need help with start-up costs and capital investment?
8. If a third-party administrator or prime contractor fails or goes out of business, is there a practical procedure for continuity?
9. Does partnership configuration require quality and nonfinancial considerations not easily allowed under government procurement policies?

integrated solution, thereby making the prime contractor responsible for nearly every facet of integration (figure 4-3). This model is particularly prevalent in the large-scale transformation efforts that require the kind of deep, best-in-class project management skills not typically found in public agencies. Often the prime contractor's valuable industry knowledge and connections equip it with the influence and expertise to forge and maintain the alliances critical to successful network management. Two huge government projects to outsource information technology (IT), the Navy Marine Corps Intranet (NMCI) and the National Security Agency's Groundbreaker, for example, both reflect the recognition that sometimes the reason for going "out to the market" in the first place is because government officials conclude that a private company can integrate and manage the various service delivery and infrastructure components better than can be done in-house.

This, at least, was the reasoning behind the decision by the city of Liverpool, England, to contract with British Telecom to coordinate all

FIGURE 4.3 **Prime Contractor as Integrator**

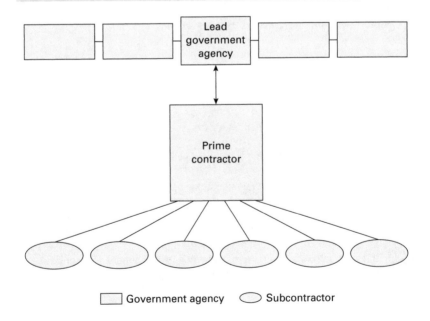

aspects of its IT modernization project, ranging from overseeing the IT investments to managing the human resources staff. British Telecom did not provide all the needed services itself. Instead it led a consortium of numerous technology providers, serving as a single source of accountability and a conduit to a host of other partners.

Agreements like that between Liverpool and British Telecom are sometimes referred to as "managed services" contracts. In these arrangements, a single prime contractor integrates a compendium of services and manages multiple subcontractors for the agency. Whereas previously the governmental entity might have purchased a range of products or services itself, under a managed services contract this responsibility shifts to the prime contractor. Government agencies in essence assume the role of consumer. As the chief knowledge officer for the Coast Guard, Nat Heiner, explains it: "You are trying to transform the delivery of information technology into a service, just like we've developed the delivery of electricity, water, telephone as services."[8]

The Transportation Security Administration (TSA) undertook this managed services approach in a very large way when it entered into a $1 billion IT managed services contract with the Unisys Corporation in 2002. Unisys manages a vendor network of at least twenty-five companies—including industry giants Dell, Cisco, Oracle, and Motorola—on behalf of the agency. Together the vendors provide all the components of the agency's IT infrastructure, including its computers, software, networks, data center, and help-desk services.

TSA adopted this model for many reasons. One was the bottom line. The agency paid less in upfront capital costs since it was buying a service rather than purchasing large-scale hardware and software. The model also enabled TSA to start up quickly after it was created by Congress in the wake of the tragedy on September 11; the agency could not have been launched as quickly if it had not relied on an experienced outside general contractor. Third, TSA needed flexibility. "So much of what we were going to need down the road was undefined" when we started, explains Pat Schambach, TSA's chief information officer. "I was lucky to know that there were 429 airports out there. But the beauty of the [managed services] model is that I just keep ordering up what I need and [the contractors] have to figure out how to provide it."[9]

Third Party as Integrator

Government officials have a third choice: hire someone solely to manage the network on behalf of the government. In contrast to the prime contractor model, the organization engaged to do this is usually not directly involved in service delivery. Instead it works on behalf of the government to optimize service delivery from the various providers, functioning as the network's broker by coordinating and stabilizing the collaborative relationships. The third-party integrator model offers governments several advantages over in-house provision. First, it allows government managers to focus more fully on policy, outcomes, and mission achievement as opposed to nuts-and-bolts operational issues. Second, outside organizations often have more tools to influence existing relationships and networks than do government organizations.

In some instances a government agency may also find the third-party integration model more fitting than hiring a prime contractor (figure 4-4). In the case of Greenwich, England, where the city council had embarked on a major modernization program involving multiple e-government providers, local officials wanted the freedom to choose best-in-class providers instead of being tied to the particular alliance partners and technologies of a prime contractor. The integrator did not come with any predetermined technology solution, giving the city council the honest broker it desired. Another important advantage of the third-party model, according to Greenwich officials, was the greater flexibility it offered: a lower initial financial commitment, shorter contract length, and greater ease of exit if something went wrong.

The state of Texas contracts with third parties to manage the state's networked model of child care, which serves more than 93,000 children. In other states the child care bureaucracy involves up to hundreds of staffers. In Texas the division managing the child care program has only fourteen employees because the state contracts for all the child care–related services it needs, including managing and evaluating the network of thousands of Texas providers that deliver child care services for low-income families in the state.

Texas does not provide any child care services itself; nor does it contract with or directly monitor day care centers. These services, as well as recruit-

FIGURE 4.4   Third Party as Integrator

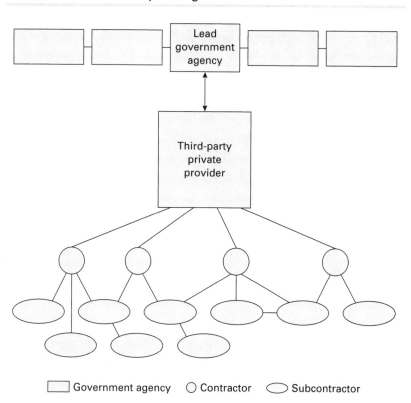

Government agency   ◯ Contractor   ⬭ Subcontractor

ing child care providers, training child care workers, providing information and resources, and assessing the performance of its network of child
care centers, are all provided by outside organizations (figure 4-5). The
state's main role is to fund the program, develop policy, and monitor the
performance of the third-party network managers.

One of these third-party administrators, Child Care Associates, is a nonprofit organization that contracts to manage child care provider networks
in several Texas counties. In the north central region of the state, for example, Child Care Associates oversees a network of more than 1,600 providers
(500 regulated child care centers and more than 1,100 licensed homes
where relatives of the children provide the care). In its role as network
administrator, Child Care Associates assesses and tracks the providers'

FIGURE 4.5   Texas Child Care Network

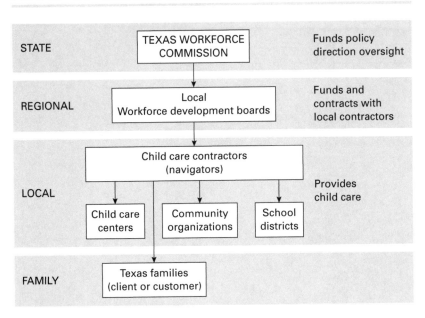

performance. In addition to this monitoring role, the organization serves both as an advocate for the parents—by providing information to families to help them choose the providers that best fit their needs and by mediating problems between parents and providers—and as a resource to providers about various types of monetary assistance.

John Whitcamp, the chief executive officer of Child Care Associates, champions the many advantages of a third-party administrator of the public-private networks. One advantage is proximity to the community. "We know who is doing what in the communities," explains Whitcamp. "We can get out into the communities to develop relationships and informal networks better than a state agency can because we are part of the communities. We're in the community every day whether it's working on welfare reform or teen parenting."

The same dynamic can be seen elsewhere in the Lone Star State. In the Gulf Coast region, the local workforce board contracts with an organization called Neighborhood Centers, Inc., to broker child care services. With roots in the settlement movement, Neighborhood Centers has been delivering an array of services to poor children since it was founded nearly a century ago. "We are just one leg of a stool that is needed to achieve a certain outcome," explains Angela Blanchard, the chief executive officer of Neighborhood Centers. "Because we all serve the same population, we have to work closely with a number of collaborative partners in the community."

The use of a third-party administrator, as contrasted to a prime contractor option, produces valuable benefits in this instance. As agents for the state, organizations like Child Care Associates allow government to devote its attention to policing and enforcing quality. This arrangement reduces to some degree the risks of failure in complex integration initiatives and makes it easier to remove and replace partners in the network. Moreover, it is sometimes helpful to have the integrator's payments set up on a different performance standard then that of the providers, thus allowing the integrator to enforce rules and penalties without consequences to itself.

Using a third party to manage the network can also have its downside, however. For one thing, it adds another layer between the government (as funder) and the ultimate client. The state of Arizona, for example, contracts with a nonprofit organization to coordinate a network of service providers for its behavioral health system. While the long-established relationships the third party has developed with the local providers play an important role in the success of this network, the system also results in five layers between the federal agency that funds the program and the provider that ultimately delivers the services.[10] Moreover, as government relies on the skills of the third-party network administrator, it runs some risk in terms of stability and continuity of institutional knowledge—although typically to a lesser degree than with the prime contractor model.

Because of the trade-offs, governments should carefully weigh a host of factors before deciding which of the three network integration models makes the most sense for their circumstances.

Deciding What Should Be Integrated

As government entities move away from a narrow, stovepipe model of service delivery, the question of what must be integrated and what can be done in pieces is an increasingly important one. In many cases, rather than outsourcing individual services to various contractors, public officials may find it more effective to link up multiple players to create a model of comprehensive service delivery. When Indianapolis subjected its airport to managed competition, for example, it first needed to determine which tasks at the airport should be included in the request for proposal and whether anyone had experience managing all aspects of an airport. The initial thinking was that the city should hire national catering companies to manage the concessions, specialized parking companies to operate the parking, and an airport operator to run the airfield activities. But after more careful analysis, the city determined that the real benefit would derive from a single organization managing all the pieces, thereby maximizing the experience for the passenger. From this model, BAA, the British company that manages Heathrow Airport and seven other U.K. airports, successfully competed for and won the contract.

As this example demonstrates, proper integration may involve meshing together the activities of a large number of entities, some of which may be other agencies and other levels of government. In cases in which close integration is required for the program to function well, breaking up the pieces into smaller contracts could cause serious—if not disastrous—operational problems later on.

The state of Kansas discovered this in 1996 when it privatized its child welfare system. The Kansas Department of Social and Rehabilitative Services divided the state into five regions and then bid family preservation and foster care separately in each region (adoption was bid out in one statewide contract). "We divided it the way we did by region and service because we wanted homegrown Kansas providers, rather than the 'big, bad managed care providers from the East' to provide the services," says Teresa Markowitz, the former department commissioner who spearheaded the privatization effort. As a result of this well-intentioned goal, a single child might be shuffled from one provider network to another several times, depending upon where the case was classified at any one time (figure 4-6). Thus the state's effort to "unbundle" the contracts inadvertently undermined one of its main policy goals: integrated service delivery.

This is not to say that a single integrated solution is always the right solution. Sometimes the government benefits by dividing the function into

FIGURE 4.6 Kansas Child Welfare Contracting Design

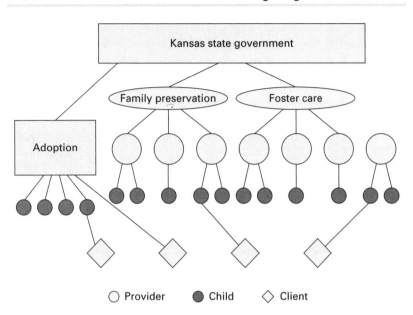

smaller contracts. Explains Alan Siu, the deputy secretary of the Hong Kong Information Technology and Broadcasting Bureau:

> In some cases, we would prefer a one-stop service, and deal with a single contractor or operator, which, of course, can engage other partners or sub-contractors. In other cases, the Government may engage more than one business partner in order to enhance competition . . . and to provide more diversified services. For example, [we have] multiple service providers in the Digital Map project of the Lands Department.[11]

Before governments turn to the market to deliver a service on their behalf, they should rigorously assess what should be kept in house, what activities should be contracted out, and how they should be bundled. To answer these questions, governments first must map out their existing processes, including all interactions between agencies, divisions, and bureaus—both with each other and with clients and citizens. A detailed discussion of process mapping is beyond the scope of this book, but when it is done right, it should help public officials to answer key integration design questions, such as:

▲ How interdependent are the current processes? What needs to stay integrated, and what can be contracted individually? The more interdependent they are, the more likely they will need to be organizationally integrated. The risk of failure increases when government breaks up the value chain of interdependent links. The unraveling of the product or service that results from nonintegrated contracts needlessly introduces risk into an otherwise appropriate outsourcing.

▲ Which processes are not "in scope" for the network solution? What processes should be retained in house and which ones should not? Governments typically do not spend enough time thinking this through during the design phase. Nor do they make the appropriate adjustments to the in-house operation to accommodate the new networked approach.

The Government Core

In this book we look primarily at networks set to accomplish public purposes, as contrasted to groups of entities, one of which is government, that coordinate their individual efforts for a specific purpose such as responding to a request by neighborhood leaders for a weekend cleanup effort. Officials must understand the limits when organizing these public purpose efforts. They need to be careful, for example, whom they invite to the table. Obviously, slumlords should not be invited to be a part of a neighborhood housing effort, nor child labor violators to a workforce training exercise.

But what about more difficult cases, where the public purpose line blurs. Should you agree to put up commercial advertising, say, Coca Cola signs, in your public playground if doing so will allow you to create twice as nice a playground? What if the partner in a major urban redevelopment project with by far the best financial offer refuses to increase its share of minority and women subcontractors? What if, in our Golden Gate Recreational Area example in chapter 1, one of the private participants was not an environmental group but an oil company willing to help the park in return for loudly publicizing the partnership? None of these questions should be showstoppers, but they demonstrate that preserving the government core includes a very difficult balancing act when the participation of network partners must be evaluated against their general reputation and their specific project requests.

Of course government may totally privatize a service and retain only regulatory participation. But in this book we look primarily to occasions where government stays actively involved and retains some responsibility. In those instances oversight is core. Even when the bulk of the integration responsibilities rests with the vendor, a government agency must still play a critical role in the overall network integration effort. Often the question of what is inherently a government responsibility revolves around labor issues and activities. For the purpose of network governance, the more relevant questions involve values: what are the core values that government must protect, and how can public officials maintain the integrity of these values in an often messy collaborative? Answering these questions requires working through important issues, such as access to services, citizen cost, fairness and equity, financial accountability, stability, and quality. When Indianapolis outsourced one of its jails, it specified minimum levels of health, food, and other necessities; the number of sheriff department employees who would always be on site; what they would inspect; and how frequently the inspections should occur. These important matters must be fulfilled by the network partners but guaranteed by government.

Protecting important values requires attention at every stage of the process, from initiation to the ongoing management of the network. A prime contractor can be required to watch these issues as they relate to the subcontractors, but that does not relieve government of its overall oversight responsibility. After hiring Lockheed to modernize its fleet, for example, the Coast Guard still employed more than fifty people to oversee the contract and coordinate with the various Coast Guard divisions. And even then the project ran into some difficulties. Only the public sector can determine policy, manage all the state-owned issues involved in the transition, and coordinate the government side of the network.[12]

To summarize the arguments made in this chapter, many of the most challenging and significant matters involved in network management concern network design: setting expectations, deciding on the most appropriate activation tools, choosing the right network structure, determining the government's role once the network has been set up, and so on. Unfortunately public officials often give short shrift to these issues. Inevitably one or two years down the line the program or service experiences major troubles caused by a poor initial design. In this chapter, we laid out a set of guidelines governments can follow when forming public-private networks. In the next chapter, we focus on how to fuse the diverse organizations of the network into a functioning whole.

CHAPTER 4—THE BOTTOM LINE

KEY POINTS

▲ The success or failure of a networked approach can often be traced to its original design.

▲ A government agency should not let its historical processes, current organizational charts, or existing capabilities dictate what activities should be pursued under a networked approach.

▲ Assets that public officials may use to activate a network include money, rhetoric, people, technology, and authority.

▲ A strong integrator is a critical component of a well-designed network.

PITFALLS

▲ Breaking up a process or program into smaller contracts when the program requires close integration.

▲ Turning over to the prime contractor matters that should be decided by the government. Only the public sector can determine policy, manage all the state-owned issues involved in the transition, and coordinate the government side of the network.

TIPS

▲ When choosing partners for the network, assess their merits based on carefully considered criteria such as values, operational capacity, reputation, and proximity to the customer.

▲ A flexible structure can help a network cope with uncertainty by allowing organizations to respond quickly to unforeseen events.

▲ Just as it often makes more sense to hire a general contractor to build a house, so too it is often in the best interests of a public agency to hire an expert to integrate the network.

EXAMPLES

▲ *Texas Child Care Network.* In many states the child care bureaucracy involves hundreds or thousands of staffers. In Texas the division managing the child care program has only fourteen employees. This is possible because the state contracts for all the child care–related services it needs, including managing and evaluating the network of thousands of providers that deliver child care services for low-income families in Texas.

▲ *U.S. Coast Guard.* When the U.S. Coast Guard sought to modernize its deepwater fleet, rather than purchasing each plane, boat, and piece of technology separately, it opted for a much different model: contracting with one consortium to replace its entire inventory as an integrated package over a multiyear time frame.

FIVE

Ties That Bind

In the last chapter we presented a framework that, among other things, helps policymakers answer the question, *Who* should integrate the network? In this chapter we will try to answer the *how* question: How do you tie together disparate organizations and discrete business processes into a functioning network? The network integrator must figure out how to establish dependable communication channels, coordinate activities between network participants, and build trusting relationships.

Technology can help. It is the central nervous system of networks, connecting partners to each other and to the public sector. For example, web-based technologies allow a third-party provider to check the eligibility of a client for job training services, a social services agency to share real-time information with its partners about an abandoned child, or a contractor delivering motor vehicle services on behalf of the state to verify instantly the identity of someone applying for a driver's license renewal.

But network integration cannot be accomplished through technology alone. It also requires addressing people issues, examining processes, aligning values, and building trust. Networks can help develop strong relationships, and strong relationships reinforce the network by building trust. Getting all these pieces right takes considerable time, skill, and, most of all, patience.

Establishing Communication Channels

As we pointed out in chapter three, communication breakdowns are a leading cause of failed networks. As service delivery shifts from in-house to network provision, the loss of informal face-to-face communication can severely disrupt the flow of information and ideas. This, in turn, can cause breakdowns in service delivery and confusion about goals and expectations. The more pronounced the cultural differences among the parties, the more important the strength of the connection.

Whether as the basis for a stable platform for ongoing projects or as the glue for first responders in emergencies, networks require free-flowing information. The United States Postal Service discovered just how critical effective communication is when it suddenly found itself overseeing the federal government's response to the anthrax crisis in 2001. Faced with managing a national security and public health crisis, the postal service developed the Unified Incident Command Center (the command center) to identify and decontaminate anthrax sites. Employees from various federal agencies as well as contractors hired to do sampling and decontamination staffed the center. It did not take long after being called in to run the command center for Paul Fennewald, from the postal service's environmental management policy department, to determine that poor information presented the most significant problem. Information was not flowing well from the postal service and the other federal and state agencies to the command center or from the command center to the outside world. "The very first thing I did is ask: What is the problem we're trying to solve here?" said Fennewald. "And I [realized] it's an information flow problem; it's a communications problem. It's not an anthrax problem."[1]

Digital Connections

In today's world, a successful network requires a digital backbone. A network can still be operated by fax, phone, and meetings, but without deep electronic links to each network partner, government management of the network is much more likely to fail.

Consider an individual infected by a bioterrorism attack. A fast and efficient response to the situation by the first responders is critical to avoid a spread of the illness. After admission to the emergency room, the patient's symptoms and eventual diagnosis must be communicated to dozens of public and private organizations involved in managing the response to the attack. Such close and rapid coordination of disparate organizations cannot be accomplished without technology that enables instantaneous communications among organizations.

With a few notable exceptions, most governments lag behind private industry in using technology to better connect with their outside partners. Today most government databases and information systems are so locked into vertical pathways that employees often cannot share information with other agencies, let alone with their partners in the private sector and the nonprofit community. The combination of vertical and horizontal information barriers inside the government agency and vertical walls between departments significantly impedes information sharing.

Rectifying this situation requires first creating an electronic gateway that allows the transfer of important information to partners in a timely fashion. Soon after first opening its doors in 2002, for example, the U.S. Transportation Security Administration (TSA) built a collaboration model that allowed rapid and secure communications among federal, state, and local governments, as well as with the agency's priority "partners" (air carriers, airport operators, external law enforcement, vendors, travel partners, and contractors). The information-sharing platform was used to supply 150 federal security directors and private vendors with consistent, up-to-date information during the rollout of the congressionally mandated federalization of security at 429 airports.[2]

TSA connects with its partners through intranets and extranets, sharing data, policies, and alerts and collaborating on projects. These collaboration technologies help the agency keep everyone in its far-flung network of federal security directors, airport administrators, air traffic controllers, and airline executives on the same page.

Similarly, twenty-two local governments in Wales use a password-protected extranet to coordinate service delivery across a wide range of government entities. To join the network, each organization must agree to an information-sharing protocol, promising to share all but the most sensitive information. The extranet site, accessed through a portal on the group's main website, provides an easy and effective way to share documents on best practices and plan for joint initiatives.

These systems allow information not only to flow freely in real time with information shared asynchronously by e-mail and threaded conversations such as electronic bulletin boards, but also synchronously through webcasts and on-line training.

Co-location

For all the advantages that modern technology provides for sharing information, nothing surpasses old-fashioned face-to-face interaction. Co-location can help revive the kind of informal communication that more often exists when all the work is done within the same organization. Most important, it can aid in building trust between individuals from the different organizations, which in turn can help build trust between the organizations themselves. To achieve these benefits, many successful public-partnerships locate at least some of their employees and operations in the same space. In Marinette County, Wisconsin, which makes extensive use of contractors for welfare-to-work services, all the parties, from senior staff to line-level employees, work side by side as a team. Eventually counterproductive public-private boundaries all but disappeared. "Being co-located is the biggest thing," says Christy Parkinsky, the director for W-2 Economic Support for Marinette County, Wisconsin. "I can just walk right over to the job manager's office when there is a problem and work through the issue with her and her staff."

In El Paso County, Colorado, providers specializing in domestic violence, developmental disabilities, child care, child support, and substance abuse have been integrated into the county's welfare-to-work network. Barbara Drake, deputy director of the county's Department of Human Services, credits co-location as being the single biggest factor causing the organizations to work together as a team. "Each partner had to co-locate an individual with authority in a central office," explains Drake. "That simple fact forced the parties to work out their differences on a daily basis."

Coordinating Activities

In addition to strong communication links, networks typically require a very high level of coordination. Consider a network developed to provide services for single low-income mothers. It might involve coordinating agencies and providers involved in everything from delivering food stamps and providing job training to arranging for day care.

Portals, middleware, and collaboration software have helped the private sector make huge strides in coordinating complex production tasks in its supply chain. Companies like Dell, Cisco Systems, General Motors, Ford Motor Company, and Herman Miller invest significant resources and executive-level attention in building electronic pipelines into their suppliers, alliance partners, customers, and employees. Rather than integrating the supply chain horizontally through acquisitions, these businesses virtually integrate with their supply-chain partners. GM Supply Power, General Motor's web-based portal, for example, links the company electronically with its suppliers, allowing them to complete transactions and share information related to purchasing, sourcing of materials, quality and production control, logistics, engineering, and manufacturing.[3] This link, in effect, eliminates the need for overstocked inventory, reduces costs, and potentially shortens the time to bring a product to market. The result? A faster, cheaper, better procurement and purchasing system.

Competing in the free market has taught the private sector that time is indeed money. Using technology to speed and improve product or service delivery enables employees of each of the organizations in the network to do more in less time, saving money. The National Aeronautics and Space Administration's Jet Propulsion Laboratory (JPL) in Pasadena, California, for example, slashed the typical design cycle for space rocket and shuttle components to two to three weeks, from eight to twelve months, by using simulation-based design and acquisition tools to collaborate with its contractors. Instead of issuing multiple RFPs and going back and forth with the contractors for months and months on each piece of the design, JPL has created an integrated mission design center packed full of computers where NASA's partners present their initial designs and requirements to NASA engineers, who then can test in real time how the design—and any modifications of it—would hold up against multiple scenarios. NASA's academic partners, other contractors, and NASA engineers are all linked up to the sessions by video conference. Not only has this innovation radically speeded up the design process, but it has also greatly enhanced the quality of the initial submissions from contractors. "If you don't have any clothes on, we'll notice real fast," explains NASA deputy chief engineer Liam Sarsfield.

Unfortunately, the sophisticated electronic collaboration tools NASA employs with its partners remain exceedingly rare in government. In fact, most agencies still interact with their partners through manual processes, creating a host of inefficiencies, from slow responsiveness and poor reliability to uncoordinated service delivery. This needs to change. Technology tools that facilitate online coordination across organizations and sectors are a necessary component of doing business. Internet-based applications now give employees from different organizations the ability to share the same workspace—even when located on opposite sides of the world. Middleware enables organizations to link up, share, and integrate information from different data computer systems. Mobile tools allow access to central office records and data systems, as well as more rapid messaging. As figure 5-1 illustrates, these and other technologies can help government organizations engaged in collaboration with others to reduce transaction costs and build trusting relationships.

Synchronized Response

These coordinating capabilities are critical for building effective public-private networks in a post–September 11 world. Take a city facing a terrorist threat to its water system. The group of individuals charged with responding to such a threat might include representatives from the Federal Emergency Management Agency, state environment officials, local hospitals, environmental groups, public utility executives, local law enforcement officers, and building inspectors.[4] A basic requirement for such a network to function would be some kind of electronic coordination mechanism that allows these disparate groups to share information in real time and synchronize their response.

The National Electronic Disease Surveillance System (NEDSS), involving forty-six states and three metropolitan health departments, provides a promising model. The goal of NEDSS, with the backing of the federal Centers for Disease Control and Prevention, is to allow participants to share information quickly so that they can identify, track, predict, and contain the spread of disease. NEDSS enables public health officials to

FIGURE 5.1   Collaboration Technologies and Organizational Performance

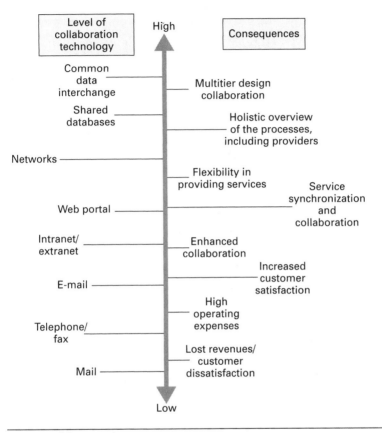

Source: Deloitte Research.

communicate public health alerts and advisories immediately. It also allows them to collect patient case data on an ongoing basis over a secure system. These data, in turn, can be used to analyze visually disease outbreaks and spread trends by neighborhood and by region.[5]

In February 2002 Pennsylvania became the first state to introduce a fully integrated disease surveillance system. More than 130 hospitals, 120 labs, 450 public health staff, and 475 physicians are connected to Pennsylvania's NEDSS (PA-NEDSS) system. So far, it has been used to report more than 100,000 cases, representing dozens of diseases in 67 counties.

Before PA-NEDSS, local health departments in Pennsylvania received reports from doctors, hospitals, and community health officials by paper and fax and then forwarded them to the state the same way—a cumbersome and slow process. It could take weeks to identify an outbreak, and by then dozens of people could have died. "The problem was the length of time it took to get something in the mail and get it to the right place for the right investigator to review it and act on it," explains Joel Hersch, director of the state's Bureau of Epidemiology. "We'd get a report a week after the lab generated it. The report would then have to be sorted and sent out to one of our investigators in the state, so it would have to be faxed or re-mailed. It could be a couple of weeks before the investigators could start checking out a situation."[6]

Pennsylvania's NEDSS changed all that. Thanks to the enhanced coordination and information-sharing capabilities, the reporting cycle of each patient case in Pennsylvania dropped from three weeks to fewer than twenty-four hours, enabling a more rapid and effective response. The system's quick detection abilities, for example, helped the York City Bureau of Health contain an outbreak of shigellosis. In another case, PA-NEDSS enabled the Bureau of Epidemiology to identify and contain an outbreak of hepatitis A. Within hours of observing the trend, officials traced the disease, notified affected parties, and closed the restaurant, in Monaca, Pennsylvania, where the disease originated.

Visibility

Coordinating activities among disparate organizations cannot occur without shared visibility into each partner's processes. Better access to information produces better decisions, which, in turn, reduce risk. To understand the benefits of visibility, consider Wal-Mart's vaunted merchandise tracking system. It connects Wal-Mart stores to their suppliers, allowing all parties to know the stores' inventory levels at any time and to order and update stock virtually automatically. Managers at Panasonic and Wal-Mart, for example, know when a stereo needs to be resupplied at a particular store. This coordinated and visible system allows Wal-Mart, its suppliers, and retail partners to make coordinated decisions about allocating resources. If a store manager does not have the desired item, he can quickly find out how to deliver it to the customer in the fastest and most effective manner, whether from a warehouse, another store, or by overnight delivery. More important, such information shared virtually instantly allows retailers and suppliers to understand demand and anticipate delivery needs.

Achieving a similar level of visibility in the public sector would have enormous benefits for networked government. A city health agency could instantly see the number of beds available in all local area hospitals that provide indigent health care services. Or a regional workforce agency could know the number and type of positions open at any given time in the job training programs of area providers. Not only would the government achieve a higher level of efficiency, but it would also provide much better and more responsive customer service.

Greater transparency would also allow a government entity to monitor services performed by contractors with the same amount of clarity and immediacy it has when it performs the service itself. How? By eliminating the asymmetry of information that exists when a vendor or subcontractor has a piece of information that the contract monitor does not have.[7] When the city of Indianapolis rebid its abandoned vehicle outsource contract, it needed to resolve a problem. It wanted to be able to locate immediately all towed vehicles in order to respond to residents asking about what happened to their cars. The solution: the city constructed an electronic pipeline into the contractors' vehicle tracking system. The vendor information system, which registered each towed car, the spot it was towed from, where it was being stored, and any subsequent moves, was available electronically to police department call takers responsible for customer service. The Arizona Motor Vehicles Department achieved a similar degree of visibility by working off the same information system as its third-party contractors, saving money by eliminating the need for establishing and maintaining records that already existed elsewhere.

Single View of the Client

Network partners also must be able to share relevant customer information in order to coordinate their activities. When a customer purchases a computer on Dell's website or makes a change in the order, all the information about her order is transmitted immediately throughout Dell's supply chain.[8] Dell's just-in-time model would not succeed if each production partner possessed a different view of the customer. Production and delivery would both take much longer.

Achieving a single view of the customer is no less important for networked government. Through CARES, Wisconsin's welfare eligibility information technology system, state employees and private contractors see the same information on their computer screens about each individual in the state's W-2 welfare-to-work program. Contractor employees also have instantaneous access to all the government information they need to do their job, including educational assessment history, state wage records, and social security records. "It allows us to work hand-in-glove with the state and county on individual cases," says Gerald Hanoski, the executive director of Workforce Connections, a welfare-to-work contractor. "It's the backbone of the network. We couldn't do our work without it."

Sadly, Wisconsin is the exception. Most governments do not share an integrated view of the customer either internally or with their partners. In Kansas's privatized child welfare system, for example, each contractor maintains its own data—little of which is tied together with data from other contractors or from the state. Keeping the records of the children up to date is a catch-as-catch-can process, involving fax, mail, and, where possible, e-mail. This enormously time-consuming and inefficient process inevitably fails as the records fall out of date and synchronization becomes impossible. "The reports come in on paper and there's no real-time reporting mechanism," says Mark Bloomingdale, chief executive officer of Lutheran Social Services, one of the contractors. "The result is a lot of duplication of effort and many data errors as the records cross over the systems."

The decentralized advantages of network service delivery also present customer management challenges. For example, an unemployed individual might enter the job training world through a neighborhood organization that invites all eligible persons in a community to walk in. If the client has a disability, he might also be involved with Goodwill Industries. If he is homeless or has a history of drug or alcohol dependency, he may also be in treatment somewhere. A single view of the client is imperative in these cases and others when governments attempt to integrate service delivery across multiple providers from the public, private, and nonprofit sectors. It enables government to apply even and fair rules to clients, regardless of their point of entry, and to make each of the various points of service more effective.

LACK OF INTEROPERABILITY. Two daunting barriers stand in the way of effective information sharing. The first is a lack of information system interoperability. Proprietary information technology systems can result in uneven communications and high collaboration transaction costs, a problem that is even more acute when some of the providers are small nonprofits. Lacking sophisticated information technology systems, these mom-and-pop organizations often struggle merely to keep up with basic paperwork, never mind integrating electronically with the government agency and other members of the network. In Texas, for example, the large nonprofit organizations that manage the child care program for the state are technologically sophisticated, but some of the child care providers do not even have Internet access. "We have a large IT staff here, but many of the vendors [child care providers] don't have a large pool of technology at their disposal," explains Angela Blanchard, chief executive officer of Neighborhood Centers, Inc., which runs the state child care system in southeast Texas. "They struggle just to maintain their basic paperwork."

The state of Oklahoma solved this conundrum. A mother can now take her child to the local child care center and swipe a state-authorized debit-like card in a point-of-service device. The child care provider learns immediately whether the state authorized the service, and the system generates a digital record that provides billing and payment support. To use the system, all the providers need is a phone line and an inexpensive point-of-sale device provided by the state. This technology makes it possible for small providers to be connected into the state's system with minimal technology, resulting in dramatically less paperwork, quicker payment, and less waste and abuse.

PRIVACY ISSUES. The second and far more formidable barrier is privacy. Integrated service delivery requires collecting, managing, and sharing information in a digital form about citizens and clients across public, private, and nonprofit providers. Information sharing across government agencies is controversial enough, but when it occurs across the public and private sector it raises huge red flags for privacy advocates. Consumer

The Indianapolis Child Welfare Collaboration System

For decades, government officials and nonprofit organizations in Indianapolis struggled to find ways to coordinate services to troubled teens. The best probation officers, child protective workers, school social workers, and juvenile police officers spent most of their time in the field with children in need of services. Although clearly the right thing to do, that practice also aggravated existing problems with service coordination as these providers engaged in time-consuming and frustrating phone tag with each other. Making matters worse, each of the public and nonprofit organizations used a separate information technology system—some of the nonprofits still used only index cards to keep track of their clients.

Top officials from all the organizations pledged to coordinate their activities, but it never really happened. Everyone knew that more information sharing meant better decisionmaking, but no one trusted the others enough to actually share information in a substantial and comprehensive way. The breakthrough finally came when, in frustration, city officials stepped in and agreed to build the necessary software and run it on its server. Middleware glued together the separate out-of-date systems, avoiding the complex, time-consuming, and expensive need to rewrite everyone into one system. All each organization had to do was sign on to a protected website. A set of rules addressed confidentiality concerns by specifying which people could see which items, thereby allowing coordinated decisionmaking while protecting the system from prying eyes.

Thus a digital tool providing instant access to a broad array of users replaced the endless search for paper documents. By taking responsibility for building the basic technical infrastructure, the city reduced the marginal cost for all the participants and greatly improved the information flow among the professionals working with children.

advocacy groups raised concerns, for example, about online tax filing being offered through third-party providers on the grounds that the information provided by the individual filer might be sold to telemarketers without the taxpayer's consent.

Public-private partnerships in sensitive areas raise privacy issues for both government and private players. Advocacy groups and the media unleashed a firestorm of criticism against both the Defense Department and JetBlue Airlines after the airline shared passenger data about 1.5 million customers with a defense contractor at the behest of the Homeland

Security Department. Complaints also caused the Transportation Security Administration to scrap its proposed Computer Assisted Passenger Prescreening System II, which would have combined information from government and commercial databases to detect individuals who might pose a terrorist-related threat. Opponents claimed that the integration of government and private sector information envisioned by the system presented a grave threat to privacy.

An exhaustive discussion of privacy in a post–September 11 world—where the barriers between public and private blur more every day—is beyond the scope of this book, but several key points provide some guidance. First, governments have been using contractors for sensitive tasks involving citizen data for decades. A rich body of knowledge has been built up on how to prevent abuses and protect privacy in situations in which a private partner is merely acting as an agent for a governmental entity, handling information belonging to the government—not the private sector—and bound by contractual restrictions. Several years ago a spate of bad publicity occurred when a private firm providing e-government services allegedly sold public data it secured as a result of its contracts with states. The resulting debate led to more careful consideration of the privacy rules contractual agents must abide by before signing any agreements.

Second, a tendency exists to find the most egregious information risk and generalize it to everyone in the network. A well-designed network can eliminate this mistaken approach by establishing a level of access highly individualized to each person of each organization, thus relieving many of the concerns. Child welfare networks, such as the Indianapolis one described above, can provide a level of information to the school social worker who is working with a particular child that differs from what it would provide to a generalized group of school administrators. Although an integrated networked model makes solving the privacy question more complicated because of the presence of multiple contractors and often multiple governments, a thoughtful design can build sufficient safeguards into the agreements.

Third, Congress and state legislators have passed laws to protect citizens' privacy. These laws will help in protecting privacy, and if they fail to prevent abuses, legislators can be expected to pass more protections. Fourth, the market itself offers some guidance. Citizens increasingly understand they must make decisions concerning trade-offs between security and privacy; the JetBlue debate, for example, exposed the company to substantial publicity that allowed its customers to hear about the issue. A private company that is perceived as abusing the public's trust on privacy matters will likely suffer bad publicity. This provides a powerful deterrent. In the end, a government official who wants to create a network can solve the privacy issues. However, without thoughtful planning, proprietary information concerns take on the appearance of serious privacy obstacles.

Building Relationships

Communicating with partners and coordinating activities provide two legs of the three-legged stool upon which network integration must stand. The third is relationship building. Sustaining a network over time and improving its capabilities requires cultivating deep ties. Creating the infrastructure and conditions that support long-term relationship building is tricky work. Integrators must devise ways to govern the network, share knowledge, align values and incentives, build trust, and overcome cultural differences.

Governance Structures

Taking a group of organizations with substantial professional differences and tacking them together at the top level is a recipe for failure. To be sure, leaders of organizations must set the stage for a successful multiparty partnership. They will not succeed, however, unless people throughout their organizations see the benefits of the network.

The first step is to set up an effective governance structure for the network. The more points of contact among the players, the more likely trust and communication will flourish. Success depends on quickly identifying and resolving any friction points. Joint governance structures that address strategy, management, and organizational activities can frame a successful network by setting out the overall vision and strategy of the network, bringing bones of contention between members of the network to the forefront early on, anticipating problem areas, and establishing a way of handling them.

Many local governments in the United Kingdom have established partnership boards to maintain direct contact between service providers and government agencies working in public-private partnerships. The boards provide a forum where government officials and their partners craft mutual objectives, articulate local priorities, and make joint decisions. Understanding that not all partner issues need necessarily to rise to a board level, some governments even created multiple layers of partnership governance arrangements. Bedfordshire, a county in southeast England, uses a partnership board, steering groups, partnership review forums, and project teams to help govern its web of partnership relationships.

Additionally, governance structures must accommodate, in advance, the need to address performance standards constantly. As we discuss in greater depth in the next chapter, performance standards are never perfect and constantly need adjustment. For example, workforce and other social service contracts often pay vendors more for work on more difficult cases. While this makes sense, differing definitions of what constitutes a difficult case and the variation in pay can produce some counterproductive results that require continuing calibration.

Governance structures also must incorporate procedures for capturing innovation and managing change. Vendors with direct, frontline relationships with clients will often see opportunities for improvement before their government managers. If the manager of the contract is a procurement official or a public employee with a more traditional hierarchical view, the suggestion often stops there since few vendors will challenge their contract manager (and thus endanger their contract) by going over his head to sell an idea. Because the very essence of the network is its dynamic, not static, nature, the relationship must be structured to harvest—not suppress—innovative ideas. Governments need to create at the outset a streamlined way to capture innovative ideas and suggestions from their partners.

Sharing Knowledge

Networks foster organizational learning. They both provide more timely access to a broader knowledge base than is possible within a single organization and help to promote the spread of successful practices.[9] Knowledge sharing, in turn, is a vital tool for integrating networks. An effective cross- organization knowledge management system can provide a host of benefits: it can help develop new knowledge, flesh out solutions to daily problems, enhance learning across the network, build trust, and help people learn from each other's successes—and mistakes.[10] These capabilities can help government to better integrate and align its own strategic objectives with those of its partners.

Two types of knowledge are generally shared between organizations: explicit knowledge and tacit knowledge. Explicit knowledge is more information-oriented and objective. It includes the kinds of facts, symbols, and data contained in manuals, websites, databases, and annual reports. Tacit knowledge, which exists within the heads of employees, is more complex and harder to codify. Born of sheer experience, it is know-how gained by practice and deliberate study, wisdom, and judgment derived from the accumulation of daily exposure to an environment. For example, tacit knowledge includes what a thirty-year veteran of government employment knows about how to navigate byzantine public sector personnel rules. Much of what you are reading in this book is tacit knowledge gained from officials with decades of experience in government, academia, think tanks, and private industry.

BARRIERS TO KNOWLEDGE SHARING. Because tacit knowledge generates innovation and competitive advantage, it provides the most value. These same benefits, however, make tacit knowledge extremely difficult to capture, transfer, and transform into action across a network. Partners, especially competitor-partners, will be reluctant to share tacit knowledge that might give their competitors a leg up against them elsewhere in the government marketplace. This is only one of several challenges to sharing knowledge across organizations. Most public agencies, nonprofits, and private companies still have not mastered how to share knowledge effectively within their respective organizations, let alone with their partners. Professional bureaucrats in rule-based systems work in well-intentioned cultures that reinforce their public responsibility to control access to important information, whether sought by another official or a citizen. This protectionism is not born of malice, or even of hopes for personal

Barriers to Knowledge Sharing

▲ Not knowing that someone has the knowledge and could collaborate
▲ Not being prepared to let people know of or share your knowledge (trust or relationship issue)
▲ Not being willing or able to capture or store knowledge (either the technology, the time, or the attitude isn't right)
▲ Not being willing to share knowledge or collaborate (fear of loss of power; no reward or incentive; not part of the job description)
▲ Not having an interest in other peoples' knowledge needs (narrow focus on personal work; no leadership commitment)

gain. Rather the hierarchy trains its armies that information can be misunderstood, or misconstrued, and therefore should be provided only in structured ways.

Hierarchical systems, stimulated by various motives, inculcate data control as part of the old governance. Professionalism often produces an arrogance that convinces officials to limit what others can see without their help. In the late 1980s, for example, when pressure began to build from employers and gun dealers for access to criminal history records held by state police departments and the FBI, those agencies resisted, arguing that data quality issues made access untenable for the untrained eye.

In the face of such barriers, knowledge sharing typically does not just happen. It requires building an infrastructure and set of routines that promote the transfer of knowledge within the network. Chief information officers can lead this charge with policy and technical suggestions, but even the line workers need to break out of informational prisons. Regular meetings, e-mail, and co-location are fairly simple mechanisms for sharing knowledge across organizations. But in today's digital age sustained knowledge sharing across organizations also requires a sophisticated technical infrastructure. Virtual communities—using technologies such as extranets, web-based seminars, electronic rooms, and bulletin boards—allow people to share information and knowledge across geographic and organizational boundaries.

The biggest benefits from "collaborative knowledge networks" will likely come from creating more interactive mediums—electronic spaces in which government agencies can communicate, collaborate, and share knowledge with their partners. Few organizations have as many interdependent moving parts as the Federal Aviation Administration (FAA). Its employees, customers, and contractors face extraordinary difficulties in coordinating projects, daily decisions, and rule making. The FAA used a variety of electronic tools to create a knowledge service network that captures knowledge across 20 business units or nodes, involving 100 work teams and 3,000 users. The information technology platform, which supports document storage, virtual conferences, scheduling, threaded discussions, and e-mail, encourages collaboration and reduces cycle times across the network. Problem-solving conferences are hosted online, and key decisions are posted on the knowledge network, replacing faxes and multiple e-mails and saving time and money.[11]

COMMUNITIES OF PRACTICE. Interactive "communities of practice" (COPs) are groups of people linked by technology and informally bound together by a common mission and passion for a joint enterprise. These communities provide another promising model for knowledge sharing. COPs can change how employees and employee groups interact with each other inside their organization and with partners and suppliers on the outside. By doing so, they produce real, quantifiable benefits for organizations. Royal Dutch/Shell Oil estimates its thirteen COPs, linking more than 10,000 users around the globe, produce at least $200 million worth of benefits for the company in knowledge transfer each year.

COPs offer a powerful, low-cost way to build trust and understanding throughout a network, and by doing so improve the overall quality of services. At the World Bank, more than 100 active COPs link bank employees and their many constituencies around the globe, allowing, for example, a staff member assisting the Nepalese Ministry of Education to easily engage colleagues in Hungary and Turkey involved in similar projects. In the past there was no way to facilitate this level of knowledge sharing.

The World Bank rates employees on their contributions to knowledge sharing in their individual performance evaluations. Bank executives evaluate managers on their ability to create an environment conducive to sharing, require experts to contribute knowledge to their respective groups, and ask employees to leverage the Bank's knowledge resources in their daily work. As a result of its knowledge transformation, the World Bank and its lending members (its "shareholders") benefit from the greater performance and value employees bring to projects. Employees benefit through greater participation in decisionmaking, and borrowing countries (the Bank's "customers") benefit through the resulting enhanced responsiveness to their needs.

Activating a community of practice and then sustaining it over time involves nourishing its key components, says COPs expert William Snyder.[12] Defining goals and then achieving short-term success builds momentum, motivates members, and provides critical energy during the early stages. Other key factors include leadership of the community and the quality of the relationships. These attributes, in conjunction with knowledge-sharing tools and practices, serve as unifying forces in a community of practice.

Creating Trust and Collaboration among Sometime Competitors

Trust is the bedrock of collaboration. Without it, people will not collaborate or share knowledge. Creating enough trust to get people to share information and knowledge, however, is extremely difficult—even when the individuals all work for the same employer. Organizational stovepipes, intradivision rivalries, and a lack of incentives to share knowledge all present formidable barriers. The task of creating trust across organizations, especially between those that may compete with each other outside the network, creates even more difficulties.[13] Yet this is precisely the challenge faced by many public-private networks. Because of the complexity of many large-scale government initiatives—which require multiple components, products, and organizations to produce a solution—large consulting firms, information technology companies, and defense contractors commonly team with one another on a project for one federal agency, while across town, at another agency, they compete vigorously against each other on another bid.

The management problems are fairly easy to handle when dealing with a network of product suppliers. The integrator suffers no loss of prestige or control by recommending one product as better suited for a solution than another. The problem becomes much more complex, however, when the solution requires a blending of the subject matter expertise of several large firms where each could conceivably be the integrator and they also compete against each other elsewhere in the marketplace.[14]

Worried about competitive advantage, these competitor-partners work hard to guard their trade secrets, proprietary solutions, and methodologies. This protective tendency, although perfectly understandable, can result in network-disrupting information hoarding. Competitor-partners may also worry about sabotage—in both more explicit and more subtle forms. "We compete with each other in other counties, but within this one we're dependent on each other for data," explains a Wisconsin welfare-to-work provider. "Another provider can take [its] time making the performance data available to you in order to make you look bad."

Even when a government official allows a third party to coordinate a network that includes its competitors, he retains substantial responsibilities. He must ensure that enough high-quality and experienced competition remains to elicit the best response in terms of price and quality. This is a fairly straightforward analysis of the competency of the remaining potential bidders.

More complicated is determining whether a consortium of providers, which compete in some areas, can cooperate successfully on the project at hand. One way to look at whether the parties can indeed work together seamlessly is to analyze whether the factors that bind them together outweigh those that push them apart (table 5-1).

Government can hire a third party to integrate the network, forcing on it the difficult task of coordinating somewhat unfriendly parties. The third-party integrator then must find a way to establish dependability, fairness, and goodwill among the organizations constituting the network. Performance measures and controls can also help, but ultimately nothing matters more than trust, a shared vision, and regular communications. "Programs slip one day at a time," explains Gene Bounds, executive vice president of operations at Robbins-Gioia, a consulting firm specializing in contract management. "They don't slip because you get 12 months down the road and find out they're behind by 10 months."[15]

By the same token, government project managers cannot abdicate their ultimate role as owner of the network. "We need to have a one-to-one relationship between a project manager and government," explains an

TABLE 5-1   Determining Whether Competitor-Partner Networks Can Work

Factors that build good partnerships	*Factors that split partnerships apart*
Partners have discrete functions	Partner-competitors doing many of the same functions
Area of cooperation is outside the business for which partners compete	Area of cooperation is in the core of each partner's business
Minimal restrictions on data sharing, or visibility into each other's data	Data carefully and narrowly shared under a tightly negotiated contract
People in charge for each company come from areas where their employers do not directly compete	People in charge for each company have directly competed in a personal way
Parties use open architecture systems	One partner uses proprietary systems or methods
Cost and pricing data are freely and continually shared	Only one partner truly understands pricing, reducing chances for smooth changes
Partners unlikely to compete again with each other using knowledge learned in current engagement	Proprietary information, if shared, would disadvantage one partner against another in the next similar procurement competition

executive at a major government information technology vendor. A point-of-contact manager, designated by the government, can improve the chances of success for a third-party private integrator working with a network that includes companies that compete in other venues. In the words of one vendor, "When we document requirements, somebody has to validate that our requirements are correct. Someone has to make sure that our performance levels are meeting government expectations. Having a government person that owns it from their perspective is a hand-in-glove fit for us. We can't work in a vacuum."[16]

The U.S. Department of Education Common Services for Borrowers project involved cooperation by otherwise competitive large vendors, such as Electronic Data Systems (EDS), Affiliated Computer Services (ACS), Pearson Government Solutions, and Raytheon. While governance issues within the vendor team are not generally an area of government scrutiny—nor should they be—the government manager needs to be confident that the team can function seamlessly. In this case, the issues between the partner-competitors concerned some competitive secrets, such as team access to proprietary source codes of individual members, but also, and perhaps more important, vital procedural matters, such as how to share management duties.

The vendors decided early on to form a truly integrated management team. Each component firm would lead in its area of expertise and manage resources from all of the other firms. They chose this approach because segregating the work would have reduced accountability and destroyed the cost advantages of the network model by causing too much duplication. An integrated team allowed for shared responsibility and a greater amount of consolidation, resulting in a better system at a better price.[17]

The same coordination issues arose in each management area, with the best legacy person selected to lead in that area, but with the team composed of individuals from multiple companies. The lesson learned was a pragmatic one: to convert a set of related systems to a truly integrated one requires a truly integrated design team using the "best-of-breed" solutions. These solutions stretched across systems, tools, and people. The software used by one partner differed from the one used by another partner, yet the team ultimately had to choose one set of tools to ensure that maintenance did not become a nightmare. This approach carried forward into operations as well. Call centers and mail houses needed to be consolidated and management teams combined, but in a way that built on institutional knowledge residing in each company's area of specialty. Trust, governance, and structural coordination all reinforced each other to blend competitors into a team on which the Education Department could depend.

Handling Cultural Differences

Integrators face a key challenge in overcoming the distrust caused when network partners possess different cultures and values. Sometimes the differences exist among the private and nonprofit partners, other times between government and its partners (where the cultural chasm is legion). In either case, the lack of trust can reduce the efficacy of the network.

The New York State Division of Parole faced this situation when it entered into a partnership with La Bodega de la Familia, a New York City community organization considered a pioneer in creating family-inclusive models for parole supervision, particularly in cases of substance abuse. The partnership was designed to reduce the number of parolees who were sent back to prison, either because they violated technical provisions of their parole agreements or because they committed more substantial crimes.

From the very beginning, substantial cultural differences caused constant tension at the seams of the partnership. For La Bodega, mission success depends first and foremost on keeping the parolee out of prison by nurturing the construction of a family-centered support network. Conversely, the parole department exists primarily to protect the public from unreformed offenders. For decades the department relied chiefly on its authority to reincarcerate parolees as its primary tool to induce individuals to reform their conduct.

Accustomed to using force, many in the parole department disparaged La Bodega's "soft" approach. La Bodega employees, for their part, criticized some of the parole department's practices—such as handcuffing parolees for minor offenses.

Rather than let these resentments fester, the partners held monthly meetings to deal with a range of issues including technical violations that should lead to arrest. The informational exchanges and policy discussions that took place at the meetings helped the two parties to better understand and respect each other's practices and viewpoints.

Shared decisionmaking also helped bridge the differences between the organizations. A signed agreement established the principles of the partnership, laid out mutual expectations, and set down a protocol for action and accountability. In the words of La Bodega director Carole Shapiro, problems occur only when one party or another exercises its authority in a noncollaborative fashion.

Also presenting integration challenges is the cultural gulf between nonprofit organizations, which tend to be fairly humanistic, and for-profit companies, which have more results-oriented and profit-based cultures. In addition to creating distrust, the cultural differences can make it hard to align values, agree on goals, and share knowledge.

As we noted previously, the 1996 welfare reform law gave states and counties the ability to engage for-profit and nonprofit partners in the effort to move welfare recipients into the workplace. Many counties and states used this new flexibility to enter into contracts with consortiums of providers to supply the full range of welfare-to-work services, including counseling, day care, job training, and placement. In these consortiums a national for-profit company often serves as the network integrator, while nonprofits function as subcontractors. Before 1996 neither the private companies nor the nonprofits had much experience working together in the welfare-to-work arena. It did not take long to figure out that they possessed very different cultures. For-profit companies had a strong cultural focus on, and sense of urgency about, getting clients into jobs *quickly*. Company profits, after all, depend to a large extent on their success in meeting targets around this measure. According to Gerald Miller, the former director of the Department of Social Services in Michigan and "father" of a now substantial private welfare-to-work business, "we instill in all our employees the belief that, when matched with the right opportunity, every client can work." Performance measures are monitored on a week-to-week or even day-to-day basis.

Many nonprofits, in contrast, looked at the issue of moving welfare recipients into work from a social services angle, focusing attention on trying to cure what they see as the pathologies that caused the clients to be in this position in the first place. They concentrated on counseling, overcoming drug and alcohol dependency, and educational programs. Many of these groups preferred the older welfare system, which did not require recipients to find a job within specified time limits and which allowed social service organizations to work indefinitely with those in need.

This difference in outlook can cause friction in the relationship between nonprofits and for-profits. Private providers view the nonprofits as having an insufficient focus on results and weak business skills. The following comment from an executive of a for-profit provider illustrates how some private providers view nonprofit management abilities: "They're not outcome-oriented. . . . There has to be a balance between the bleeding-heart social worker who wants to do the right thing and the business side. We have that balance. We care very much about the people we serve—it's our priority. But we do it with good business sense. Most not-for-profits just don't think that way."

The real or perceived cultural differences between the two sectors often shape the structure of collaboration in welfare services. Contrary to what these comments suggest, the for-profit integrators did not use their leverage to induce the nonprofits to mirror more closely the for-profit culture and strategic objectives. Instead of trying to meld these very different cultures, the for-profit integrators generally assign nonprofits ownership over areas in which they can add value without diluting the for-profits' focus on results. The result: nonprofits own tasks like outreach, organizing job fairs, conducting home visits, arranging for child care, and providing special services for certain immigrant populations, while the for-profits retain the core responsibilities of job training and job placement. Explains an executive from a for-profit provider:

> Say you're a nonprofit. I'm going to pay for one full-time staff person. You're going to get a desk and a computer. And I'm going to house you in my facility, and you are now a member of our staff. The person walking through the door doesn't know if you work for the Neighborhood House or the Urban League. And here's what you've got to do. First, you're responsible for making my generalist case managers significantly aware and appreciative of your client population. I'm not going to be able to train my managers to treat domestic violence and they shouldn't need this specific expertise. . . . So you show us and train us how to recognize problems and when to refer people to you.

For-profits also frequently deal with cultural differences by limiting the types of staffers allowed to work on the premises of the welfare office. In particular, many of the for-profits want only nonprofit staff that share their confidence in the ability of their clients to work. "We don't deal with 'enablers'; we deal with solutions-based folks," explained a manager at one for-profit firm. "If you're a nonprofit and you send an 'enabler' into our office, we'll say 'can you give me a solutions-based person?' I have yet to know of an organization that doesn't want to have the same sense of urgency [as we do], but it may not have been exposed to a structure that would allow them to do it."

Not surprisingly, many of the nonprofit providers view things differently, believing that sometimes the for-profits do not pay enough attention to the unique needs and characteristics of the individual clients. For example, the director of one nonprofit provider argued that case managers at the for-profit integrator ignored the initial client assessment and, as a result, encouraged clients to seek jobs in fields that did not match their qualifications. He encouraged the firm to modify its approach, which it eventually did: "It took a while, and a lot of training on our part, to get the staff [of the for-profit] . . . to see the benefit of using this information.

But finally, now, they've started to say 'This person has some physical limitations; we need to look for a more sedentary occupation for her.' Or, 'This person has skills in computer occupations. This is going to be a good job match.'"

All in all, in most of the welfare-to-work consortiums we examined, the integrator, usually a for-profit company, or in some cases a large national nonprofit like Goodwill Industries, carefully placed the smaller nonprofits inside the larger mission set by the new law and the contracting local government agency. The government by this structure could hold one entity responsible for a series of performance outcomes—and avoid a situation where centrifugal forces in the network blurred the clarity of the performance goals.

Information technology can help tear down the walls between organizations, giving governments and their private-sector partners the tools to work effectively across their organizational boundaries. Billing, finance, purchase orders, and other financial transactions can be automated, saving time and money. Best practices and lessons learned can be exchanged across organizations to enhance effectiveness. Organizations in different locations can collaborate on projects and documents in real time. All network partners can share a single view of the customer to serve her more efficiently. But at the end of the day, technology is only an enabler. It cannot solve the problems of building trust between organizations. It cannot get organizations with very different values and cultures to collaborate and share knowledge. These and many other challenges of integrating networks require creative and skilled people with the vision and know-how to bring together multiple organizations across sectors into a functioning whole.

CHAPTER 5—THE BOTTOM LINE

KEY POINTS

▲ Integrators must devise ways to establish communication channels, coordinate activities between network participants, share knowledge, align values and incentives, build trust, and overcome cultural differences.

▲ Trust is the bedrock of collaboration. Without it, people will not collaborate or share knowledge.

▲ Technology can help organizations collaborating with others to reduce transaction costs and build trusting relationships.

PITFALLS

▲ Uneven communications and high collaboration transaction costs caused by incompatible, proprietary information technology systems.

▲ Cultural differences that make it hard to align values, agree on goals, and share knowledge.

TIPS

▲ Promote trust and better communication by establishing more points of contact among the network partners.

▲ Bring bones of contention between members of the network into the open early on in the collaboration by creating joint governance structures.

▲ Bridge differences between organizations through shared decisionmaking.

EXAMPLES

▲ *NASA's Jet Propulsion Laboratory.* NASA slashed the typical design cycle for space rocket and shuttle components to two to three weeks, from eight to twelve months, by using simulation-based design and acquisition to collaborate with its contractors.

▲ *Pennsylvania's National Electronic Disease Surveillance System.* Users can share information quickly and identify, track, predict, and contain the spread of disease. The result? The disease reporting cycle dropped from three weeks to less than twenty-four hours, enabling a more rapid and effective response.

▲ *CARES, Wisconsin's welfare eligibility information technology system.* State employees and private contractors can view the same information on their computer screens about each individual in the state's W-2 welfare-to-work program.

SIX

Networks and the Accountability Dilemma

I t did not take long after the space shuttle *Columbia* exploded in mid-flight for people to start pointing fingers in all directions. Since 1996 United Space Alliance, a Houston-based partnership between Boeing and Lockheed Martin, operated many space shuttle functions, including training and some safety responsibilities. With two of the world's largest aviation and defense contractors, as well as the National Aeronautics and Space Administration itself, all playing important roles in the space shuttle program, no one seemed to be able to sort out responsibility for the disaster.

Should NASA be held responsible because its senior managers failed to heed the prescient warnings of their engineers? Is Lockheed Martin to blame because it built much of the shuttle? Is Boeing, Lockheed's partner in the Space Alliance, at fault because it advised NASA during midflight that no serious problems would arise from the large chunk of foam that broke off from the external fuel tank during the takeoff and struck the left wing of the aircraft? Or does responsibility belong to a combination of the three?

The accountability problem presents networked government with its most difficult challenge. When authority and responsibility are parceled out across the network, who is to blame when something goes wrong? How does government relinquish some control and still ensure results?

How do network managers balance the need for accountability against the benefits of flexibility?

Although private sector companies have struggled for years to answer these questions, governments face a host of unique challenges that extend well beyond those of the private sector. Outcomes in government are often murky, hard to define, and harder to measure—and may take many years to realize. Moreover, when something goes wrong in a public sector network, it tends to end up on the front page of a newspaper, instantly transforming a management issue into a political problem.

The good news is that the very act of creating a network draws much more attention to accountability then simply maintaining an existing government bureaucratic delivery system. There are, of course, efforts to measure performance in a government bureaucracy—the federal government's Performance Accountability Rating System and the Government Performance Results Act, to name two—but often these efforts have little or no connection to whether a government bureau stays in business or how a government employee is compensated. With public-private networks, in contrast, accountability typically involves the ultimate question of whether the network continues at all, thus focusing the mind greatly. The bad news is that defining, measuring, and rewarding performance is very difficult stuff, with ample opportunities for mistakes and embarrassment before one sees results.

Key to unraveling the accountability conundrum is understanding the hierarchy of responsibility. Who should be held accountable, and by whom? If the government is the general contractor and one subcontractor hinders others' performance, who should be held responsible? Or in the case of a private integrator, should the government procurement manager care how the private integrator treats its subcontractors, how it holds them accountable, and for what? When federal government agencies delegate to a city or state the right to make grants with federal dollars, to whom are the grantees accountable?

Governments have traditionally tried to address most of these issues of governance and accountability through narrow audit and control mechanisms (table 6-1). Although such tools help, they should not constitute the greater part of an accountability regime. An overreliance on box checking

TABLE 6-1   Accountability Models

Type of accountability	Finances	Equity/ quality	Performance	Trust	Incentives
Traditional	Standard, prescriptive, record-keeping	Compliance with program rules	Compliance with input and record-keeping	Low	Cost-plus
Hybrid/ transitional	Proof of dollars for contracted services only	Rules emphasizing fairness and equity	Activities	Medium	Fixed price
Flexible network	Proof of performance	Service-level agreements	Outcomes	High	Penalties and rewards tied to results

and rule compliance—in which government contract monitors focus on finding wrongdoing instead of making the partnership work—leads to an adversarial relationship with partners. Network partners, faced with intrusive and frequent performance and price audits, tend to become rigid and risk averse. Innovation collapses and trust suffers, reducing the essential value of the relationship. Additionally, traditional accountability mechanisms, which rely on process standardization, clash with the very purpose of the network: to provide a decentralized, flexible, individualized, and creative response to a public problem.

The experience of the Corporation for National and Community Service (CNCS)—the quasi-government parent agency of national service programs including VISTA and AmeriCorps—demonstrates these problems. CNCS provides college scholarships and stipends to individuals who participate in a broad array of community work, ranging from small neighborhood and faith-based groups to national organizations such as Habitat for Humanity and Teach for America. About half the corporation's funding flows through state governments and then to the organizations supporting, say, the AmeriCorps member; the other half comes directly from the federal government.

Repeated problems led Congress to demand more accountability from AmeriCorps and other CNCS programs. In 2001 the CNCS inspector general interpreted this request for accountability to mean detailed audits of the community organizations receiving state grants to deliver services and employ AmeriCorps members. Difficulties quickly arose because the small nonprofits did not adequately document their time and procedures and thus compliance was difficult to prove. Furthermore, although only a few entities actually had any financial problems that warranted investigation, many did not have the documentation necessary to back up their results. A relatively small inspector general's staff quickly became overwhelmed in detail, unable to distinguish real fraud or structural problems from technical issues. As with any sprawling enterprise, some grantees abused the system, but in this case the entire network's flexibility was compromised once the accountability enforcers became increasingly prescriptive on issues such as record-keeping. These difficulties snowballed when process and accounting errors on the part of CNCS—the network activator, funder, and monitor—caused enormous harm and rippling trauma for the grassroots network members.

Even after CNCS responded to pressure from the inspector general, the White House Office of Management and Budget, and the General Accounting Office to improve its historically weak internal procedures, difficulties persisted. Former director Les Lenkowsky commented that despite controls to reduce fiscal problems, the lack of uniform performance criteria made it impossible to determine whether taxpayers actually got results from the funding. The accountability scheme ensured that blatant financial errors were corrected, but it produced little data on whether the dollars actually accomplished anything.

Getting results from networks requires a comprehensive framework that contains a set of strategies for addressing the following seven areas crucial to accountability: setting goals, aligning values, establishing trust, structuring incentives, measuring performance, sharing risk, and managing change (figure 6-1). Within these and other areas—such as financial performance—it is also important that an effective network accountability structure follow a broader, more flexible approach than is typical in traditional approaches to accountability (see table 6-1).

FIGURE 6.1 Accountability Framework for Networks

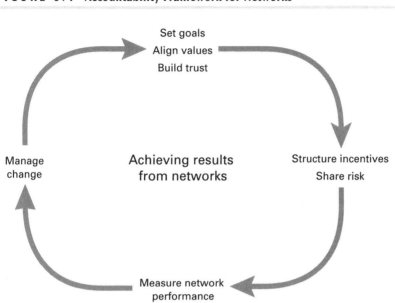

Setting Goals

When government brings together network participants to accomplish a goal, the individual aspirations of the participants must be carefully aligned both with each other and with the broader goal. Alignment requires clear, ambitious, and outcome-based performance targets that support the overall strategy of the network. Such targets clarify for participants exactly what needs to be accomplished and supersede the competing interests and priorities of participants from varied backgrounds.

The first step in setting useful targets is determining what the government-initiated network needs to accomplish. To do this, network architects must define the public good they want to produce; the services and outputs they want to provide; and the goals the network should accomplish. Thus network expectations must be specific enough to enable the actors to deliver services effectively but flexible enough to avoid saddling participants with detailed procedures for achieving these outcomes. This emphasis on clarity moves the initiator-participant relationship from an adversarial one to a cooperative one with shared goals.

Two specific steps help network architects align goals and establish clear and achievable performance targets: seeking input from network participants regarding goal setting and targets, and then pushing the shared goals and targets down to all levels of the network.

Seeking Input

Seeking feedback from potential or current network members and stakeholders helps to avoid a situation in which government sets unrealistic outcome goals that in turn can cause a general lack of acceptance of the goals and performance standards from the participants in the network. The importance of seeking input was borne out by the city of Liverpool, England, when it sought to comply with the United Kingdom's Local Government Act, a statute that required local authorities to produce a strategy for improving the economic, social, and environmental well-being of their communities. The city government responded to the Local Government Act by forming the Liverpool Partnership Group. Consisting of twenty-three member organizations and more than a hundred participating organizations along the entire spectrum of community, business, and social service groups, as well as the city council and government agencies, the Liverpool Partnership Group has become a model for community networks in the United Kingdom. Feedback on proposed goals, priorities, and performance targets comes from the bottom up, through local forums, focus groups, and neighborhood action plans, rather than from the top down. The overall community strategy, called Liverpool First, ensures continuous alignment of the goals and performance targets through cycles of direction-setting and feedback.

In addition to the benefits of broad involvement, Liverpool First illustrates the importance of input-based flexibility. For example, after criticism that the Liverpool Partnership Group's subcommittees tended to be "talking shops" that resulted in vague performance targets, the city implemented measures that made the partnership groups more oriented to action and outcomes. A little more than a year after the early criticism, the municipality had accomplished on schedule 61 percent of the 171 initiatives outlined in the Liverpool First strategy, 34 percent had experienced some delays, and a mere 5 percent had been abandoned.[1] One major success was a joint venture with British Telecom to modernize the city's outdated information technology systems.

Pushing Goals Down the Network

Even more challenging than creating and aligning goals is figuring out how to push them down the network. It is a particular conundrum for programs where a federal manager is often four to five levels removed from actual service delivery but nonetheless remains accountable for program performance. The federal manager must somehow find a way to ensure attention to the performance goals and incentives all the way down to the service delivery level while imposing a minimum of burden on the intervening layers.

The further away a program is from the source of funding the more difficult it is to achieve goal clarity. In these cases, governments rarely even *try* to push goals down a network—and even more rarely do they get it right. For example, in 2002 when the Bush administration began assessing federal program performance as part of its budget and performance integration project, the Office of Management and Budget could rate only 50 percent of the programs. The reason? Insufficient data about program results. No one could really say for sure whether the programs produced tangible outcomes. Tellingly, a significant number of these programs were delivered by third parties—some by state and local governments and some by contractors.

The Wisconsin W-2 case discussed in chapter two provides one example in which all levels of the network fully understood the public sector goals. The broad congressional goal of moving people from welfare into the workforce—together with the requisite incentives for good performance and penalties for poor performance—cascaded down from the federal level to the state level to the local providers. In this instance, pushing down the goal worked for several reasons: the presence of clear and well-publicized federal goals, alignment at all levels regarding goal worthiness, and strong financial incentives for achieving the goals.

In addition to ensuring that these three elements are in place, getting buy-in to the goals at the beginning can help rally people around them later. Mayor Anthony Williams of Washington, D.C., enlists several thousand city residents to participate in citizen summits designed to *create* goals for the city. These goals act as motivators for city agencies to involve the community groups in helping the agencies, and therefore the city as a whole, achieve the goals. As Williams describes the process:

> I've had two citizen summits. We've had about 4,000 people at each summit. They set major goals for the city, which we translate into a performance plan for the city and for individual neighborhoods. We use it to organize agency services at a neighborhood level. It's all metric based. An example would be . . . after-school programming. There is a goal for the deputy mayor for children, youth, and families; there's a goal for the director of parks and recreation for these kinds of programs. At the same time, the faith community helps contribute to that goal.

Aligning Values, Creating Trust

Accountability within a network cannot be composed wholly of a series of contract clauses. Successful networks rely, at least partly, on trust. Without trust, network participants are unwilling to share knowledge, hindering coordination between them. Conversely, networks operating with a high level of trust lower the costs associated with interorganizational exchanges (table 6-2). These "oversight costs," include all costs related to procurement, search, and third-party monitoring. When trust is absent, oversight tends to be high, reaching anywhere from 35 to 40 percent of economic activity costs in low-trust situations.[2] Government officials, forced to spend inordinate amounts of time negotiating,

TABLE 6-2   The Value of High-Trust Relationships

	High trust	Low trust
Contract oversight	Flexible Outcome-based oversight Constant modifications to capture value	Tight Input audits Intrusive and frequent output exams Rigidity on modifications
Value equation	Low cost, high value	High cost, low value

monitoring, and enforcing inflexible contract provisions, drive up over-head costs.[3]

High trust levels reduce oversight costs by encouraging more open infor-mation exchange, which removes dependence on costly legal approaches to solving relationship issues. How can network architects encourage trust-based relationships among partners? For one thing, they must clearly communicate the values and goals of the network at the outset of the rela-tionship. This entails building appropriate governance structures during the early stages of contract negotiation to handle risks, rewards, benefits, and opportunities. Early attention to structure reduces the possibilities of major misunderstandings later in the relationship.

For example, when the United States Navy entered an $8 billion part-nership with Electronic Data Systems to build the Navy Marine Corps Intranet, both parties worked diligently to achieve a shared understand-ing of the goals—testing assumptions—before writing the contract. "Both parties [need] to understand at the conceptual level the goal that has to be reached," says former NMCI director Rear Admiral Charles Munns. "Once you have that shared understanding, you can recognize some of the weak-nesses and ambiguities in the contract, put each one on the table, and talk through it." Although, as described later, EDS accepted responsibilities that proved problematic.

When government assembles a network of partners based solely on lowest-cost bids and gives little heed to whether government and its part-ners have a shared understanding of common values and goals, serious problems can ensue. That was the result of an ill-fated education man-agement contract between Hartford (Connecticut) City Schools and Edu-cation Alternatives Incorporated (EAI), an education management firm. EAI and the Hartford school district mutually ended their contract after only sixteen months. The partnership failed in large part because the two parties had very different notions of the desired outcomes. Specifically, the contract stipulated that Hartford would pay EAI from any savings that the company could generate for the school district. The contract ran into difficulty, however, because the school district and EAI could not agree on what actually constituted a savings. "What did the experiment in was a lack of specificity about roles, responsibilities, payments, and outcomes," says John McLaughlin, an expert on education privatization.[4]

A relentless attention to choosing participants with shared values creates both the cohesion and framework necessary to produce a true partnership. But no matter how carefully a government agency chooses its partners, time should be set aside early in the contracting process to align values and create trust.[5] Network architects can facilitate early-stage trust building and goal alignment by making the central goal so clear and compelling that the inherent centrifugal forces will not overwhelm its structure.

The 1996 welfare reform law transformed welfare from handouts to a work-based benefit. Before then, social service providers offered services for a fee, and local governments, United Way, or foundations would grant on the same condition: fee for service. But then new welfare-to-work networks built in Florida, Texas, Wisconsin, and several other states required providers to buy into the new culture of work with performance measured in jobs, not counseling sessions.

Although drug therapy obviously was still necessary in some cases, it had to be provided by a network partner as a step toward the self-sufficiency produced by a job. States engaged private integrators to create performance-based systems centered on supporting participants' ability to work, not subsidizing the continuing amelioration of their pathologies. Subcontractors and team members needed to agree with the organizing philosophy that almost all individuals were capable of work and the self-respect that goes with it.

The integrator needed to insist that partners learn to value the centrality of work and self-sufficiency regardless of their existing worldview. In other words, the enactment of a very specific legislative goal compelled many public agencies to seek to reduce their risk of failure by selecting partners whose cultural values already coincided with the new legislative goal. The new delivery systems included only partners whose assigned employees believed everyone they touched was capable of obtaining employment in a relatively short period of time.

Structuring Incentives

Incentive structure is also crucial; it can make the difference between a network that succeeds and one that fails.[6] Consider the Medicare program—a veritable case study on the influence of skewed incentives. Fraud and abuse cost taxpayers an extra $50 billion to $75 billion annually, according to Harvard professor Malcolm Sparrow.[7] Not surprisingly, it turns out third-party administrators lack incentives to police the providers adequately. When it created Medicare in 1965, Congress compromised with the health care establishment: doctors and hospitals would participate in the program only if they could select the insurance companies that would process the claims and serve as program watchdogs. Paid a fixed price for each claim processed, Medicare contractors have a strong incentive to process them as cheaply as possible. According to the General Accounting Office, standard insurers typically allot the claims review process more than 8 percent of the total cost of paying claims. Medicare processors, however, spend only 0.007 percent of the total Medicare claims-processing cost on ferreting out fraud and abuse. As an official at one California insurer put it, "We try to do a good job, but we don't get extra money for doing a good job."[8]

Without question there are well-meaning bureaucrats managing competent and honest Medicare processors. But what gets measured and rewarded gets done. When the contract manager rewards an activity, the contractors will produce more of the same, and in the case of Medicare, the rewarded activity is paying claims on a transaction basis, not producing better health care per dollar spent. The point of this illustration is not to critique how the Medicare program measures performance, but rather to emphasize that well-structured incentives must lie at the heart of network governance. Yet they are difficult to achieve—especially when the network has multiple partners.

As this example demonstrates, badly structured incentives can have unintended influences on the performance of a network. Financial incentives should be structured to encourage quality, cost savings, creativity, innovation, and continuous improvement. Partners can be rewarded for meeting milestones, penalized for failing to do so, and even paid a percentage of savings at the end of the job. Incentive-based arrangements must be structured not only to save money, but also to improve quality. That is easier said than done. Government's failure to capture fully and accurately its own costs or to measure rigorously the performance of its own programs are just two of the challenges to structuring performance incentives.[9] Four guidelines, described below and summarized in the accompanying box, can help meet the challenge of tying incentives to goal achievement.

Tie Incentives to Results

Tying partners' payments to the achievement of specified results helps to maintain partner-government goal alignment. Financial rewards and penalties can be tied to a wide array of performance goals depending on the priorities of the agency. Several local governments in the Netherlands joined together to improve safety and reduce congestion on a dangerous secondary road (N50) near Den Bosch. The governments, to achieve these goals, contracted with a private consortium to convert the road into a highway through a design, build, and operate arrangement. The payments over the eighteen-year life of the contract are tied directly to certain quality thresholds, such as the smoothness of the road and how much of the highway is fully available for use at any one time. "This project means a new way of cooperation between public and private parties," explains project director Piet Wouters. "It demanded a mindshift for all parties. Responsibilities and risks are shared in a very different manner, which requires a different way of working."

In chapter three we discussed how vital it is to have good baseline numbers on service costs and quality before tendering a service to the private sector. This is particularly true for performance-based partnerships. The absence of good baseline data about current services, as well as projections for future costs, often causes one of two things to happen: the private sector realizes politically unacceptable windfall profits on the project or alternately loses large amounts of money. Electronic Data Systems, for example, took more than $1 billion in losses on its contract to build the Navy Marine Corps Intranet (NMCI), causing EDS's stock to plummet. Both the Navy and EDS grossly underestimated the number of antiquated computer systems that needed upgrading, thus producing huge financial losses.[10]

While having good baseline numbers is critical for getting the initial targets right, it is not sufficient to guarantee success. Time and time again we discovered that even the most well-designed, results-based contractual approaches ran into serious problems. Shifts in economic conditions,

Guidelines for Structuring Meaningful Incentives

Government network designers should keep in mind four guidelines for structuring incentives for network partners:

▲ Tie incentives to results, rather than activities
▲ Beware of creaming—the practice of skimming the easiest cases and leaving the difficult ones for other partners to handle
▲ Share the savings gained from operating more efficiently
▲ Seek reasonable performance guarantees to ensure that partners will be accountable for their actions

increases in the client base, statutory changes, or a host of other factors conspired to render the initial performance goals inappropriate or unattainable. The state of Wisconsin found this out the hard way when it privatized welfare delivery and administration in Milwaukee. To encourage continuous improvement, the state structured performance goals to force partners to meet progressively higher targets each year, a good idea except the initial benchmarks were set too low. Wisconsin officials quite understandably failed to anticipate the huge and rapid reduction in the welfare rolls caused by the reformed welfare system. As a result the contractors did too well financially during the initial years, causing some really bad press and serious legislative concern. "We did not anticipate well," says a Wisconsin official.

Just when the state emerged from this controversy, the tougher performance targets kicked in, but unfortunately they hit right in the middle of an economic downturn. Not only did the very depressed labor market make the tougher targets challenging, but even more important, the welfare recipients remaining to be placed in jobs were by far the most difficult to place. The goals proved unattainable. "I don't know of a single W-2 operation in the state of Wisconsin that can make it through the two-year contract period in terms of dollars," said Jerry Hanoski, who runs an agency overseeing W-2 in six counties. "It's a statewide issue, and it's a train wreck waiting to happen."[11] We talk more about how to guard against such predicaments later in the chapter when we discuss how to manage change.

Beware Creaming

As the case study of Oklahoma's Community Rehabilitation Services Unit (CRSU) described in the box on pages 136–37 illustrates, when pay is connected to performance, public officials need to guard against creaming—the tendency of some providers to compete with each other for the "easiest" cases.[12] The Family Partnership Initiative in Wisconsin, a fourteen-county consortium created for the purpose of contracting for child welfare services in rural Wisconsin, addressed creaming by choosing a respected organization to oversee the other providers. Lutheran Social Services, the network manager, created a risk pool from its county payments to allow it to better manage difficult cases. The incentives encouraged and rewarded those providers who devoted significant efforts to helping the hardest to serve.

Share in Savings

To mitigate incentive structure difficulties, network architects may opt to negotiate a guaranteed savings level from contractors and then share any additional savings. This approach gives partners a powerful incentive to reduce costs consistently over time. For example, in 1995 BAA USA won a bid to manage the Indianapolis International Airport, making it the largest privately managed airport in the United States. BAA guaranteed the city annual savings of $2.5 million before the company could realize any profit. Each and every year, BAA exceeded its guarantee. After the guaranteed savings, the city also received 60 percent of any additional savings the first year and a higher percentage in later years. Even a straightforward guarantee like the one between BAA and Indianapolis, however, can face extraordinary pressures. The September 11 terrorist attacks changed the environment for airports, adding security and changing parking among other things, all of which made administering the contract very difficult.

As appealing as shared savings approaches can be for cash-strapped governments, they are not easy to get right. If structured poorly, they encourage cost cutting at the expense of service quality, distort behavior, limit the pool of potential vendors, or even bankrupt partners.[13] Following a few basic rules can improve the odds of success. In addition to getting the baseline data right, all parties must clearly understand the objectives, agree on the performance metrics, and create a governance structure that allows for midstream changes when needed.[14]

Seek Performance Guarantees

Buying outcomes, when possible, clearly is preferable to paying for inputs. Yet sometimes only activities, and not outcomes, can be managed. Historically in road construction contracts, government buys cubic yards of concrete, or so much reflector material. When a state hires a company to build a road, it appears to be purchasing quantities of time and material. But not to Peter Rahn, the former head of the New Mexico Department of Transportation. For the 125-mile road-widening project on New Mexico's Corridor 44, Rahn rejected the traditional method of hiring one contractor to build the road and then hiring others over time to maintain it. Rahn asked, "Why can't the contractor that builds the road also be held responsible for maintaining it for a specified period of time?" After all, Rahn reasoned, if he could get a five-year service warranty on a new refrigerator from Sears, why could he not do the same when he purchased a road?

It turns out he could. Despite grumbling from some road contractors who hated the idea, Rahn entered into an agreement with Koch Performance Roads to provide something called a "pavement warranty," a contractual guarantee that the road will function appropriately for, in this case, twenty years. If it does not, Koch has to replace or repair the road surface at no cost to the Department of Transportation.

The warranty provides a powerful incentive for the contractor to build the original road in the highest-quality fashion so it will last a long time. In this case, New Mexico expects the road's pavement serviceability rate, or road quality, to be 4.5 on a scale of 0 to 5, at all times.[15] The warranty contract will save the state $89 million in highway maintenance costs over

Oklahoma Milestones

From 1985 to 1991 Dan O'Brien managed the Red Rock Mental Health Center in Oklahoma, a "supported employment" service that helps citizens with profound disabilities secure lasting employment. Red Rock and other vendors provided these services under contract to the state's Community Rehabilitation Services Unit (CRSU). As soon as O'Brien went to work for the State of Oklahoma in 1991, he began making his case that the state's "twisted incentives" distorted network providers' results.

The twisted incentives problem that O'Brien articulated is found in many government agencies: the state was paying for activities, rather than outcomes. Under the program, twenty vendors provided individual job coaching services to a client base of about 500; the coaches traveled with clients to the job, often accompanying them for extended periods of times while the client sought for and became acclimated to the new job. CRSU paid hourly wages for these coaching services, so billable time, not client service, became the goal.

By 1991, when O'Brien came on board, the average number of days to a successful placement and case closure had swelled to 483. CRSU did not terminate vendors for low levels of placement so long as they sufficiently documented their activities with the clients they were helping. Indeed good vendors suffered because they lost a source of revenue if they placed a client in a job quickly.

To remedy this systemic problem, O'Brien suggested that CRSU radically restructure its incentives: pay vendors when they accomplish certain milestones and prohibit agencies from billing for a milestone more than once per client. The final milestone—permanent placement of a disabled citizen in a job—carried the largest payment. This way the vendor incentives would be more closely aligned with the state's goal of long-term employment for the disabled.

twenty years, according to the department. Moreover, monitoring the contract is more straightforward and less expensive than measuring and inspecting each component.

Sharing Risk

Networked arrangements allow financial, performance, and even political risk to be transferred to the private and nonprofit sectors. For example,

Oklahoma Milestones (*Continued*)

When O'Brien first proposed incentive restructuring, he encountered significant opposition. Some vendors, for example, suggested that others might try to cream the most employable clients off the top of the list, neglecting the extremely disabled clients who were likely to be harder to place. In response O'Brien redesigned his proposal to pay more for the placement of the most-challenged clients. Still, anxiety and opposition continued. Many vendors had never put together a budget. Job coaches worried that some of their clients would fail at work without their help. Some public officials worried—reasonably enough—that job placement as the main performance criterion would reduce the availability of important mental and social services.

Despite these concerns, the restructuring worked. After implementation, many program managers and job coaches said the milestones gave them greater flexibility. Before the restructuring, the state had specified the allowable number of job coaches; under the new system, managers could make such decisions themselves. And instead of documenting fifteen-minute activity intervals, vendors began to focus on outcomes. Many job coaches placed their clients within weeks—not months—and they doubled and tripled annual case closures. As a safeguard, CRSU tied vendor payments to whether the client liked the job, reducing the chances of impersonal and inappropriate placements. Six months after implementing the new incentives, fully 81 percent of the field staff working for network partners thought CRSU's quality of service had improved.

Because no performance standard is ever perfect, some hard-to-help individuals undoubtedly fell through cracks in the job-placement system. Despite natural limitations, the new incentive structure enabled exponential improvement in CRSU's outcomes, which ultimately translates into better service for Oklahomans with disabilities.

incentive-based contracts can shift much of the risk to a contractor, rewarding it for productivity improvement and penalizing it for poor performance or rising costs. This was the case in California following the 1994 Santa Monica earthquake. The California Department of Transportation contracted with a highway construction company to rebuild a highway overpass and offered substantial performance incentives and penalties: a $200,000 a day bonus for completing the project ahead of schedule and a $200,000 penalty for each day the project ran behind schedule.

The Special Challenge of Imposing Consequences on Nonprofits

"Networked government produces a special challenge in acting on poor performers," asserts Leslie Lenkowsky, former CEO of the Corporation for National and Community Service. "It's often more difficult to reduce funding based on poor performance." Indeed, nonprofit organizations working in a government-initiated network tend to be prominent in their communities. Thus when they perform poorly, their visibility makes it politically difficult for governments to impose tough consequences—especially contract termination. Nonprofits also lack the profit motive, which means there is less of an economic incentive for good performance than is the case with for-profits.

When outsourcing fails in the private sector, the fault almost invariably lies with both the vendors and the contract manager. That also holds true in government-managed networks. Thus when the government attempts to discipline a respected grassroots organization for not upholding responsibilities in a network relationship, the government's reasoning must be clear and free of politics and self-interest. Otherwise the organization is likely to fight the disciplinary action by seeking support from the legislative branch.

CNCS attempted to change its model of doing business and impose accountability on nonprofits at the same time that the long-standing weakness of its central office management became a visible and important issue. In that weakened environment, what might have passed for reform when the corporation was favorably perceived became instead a rallying cry for opponents of the reforms to take to Congress. The effective reach of the

Because of the streamlined contracting process, repair work began the day after the January 17 earthquake. The financial incentives resulted in the overpasses being replaced in a little over two months, seventy-four days ahead of the June 24 deadline. To complete the project so early, the contractor worked crews around the clock, using as many as four hundred workers a day. The $74 million in savings to the local economy and $12 million in contract administration efficiencies thanks to the shortened schedule more than offset the $13.8 million the contractor received in performance bonuses.[16]

The Special Challenge of Imposing Consequences on Nonprofits
(*Continued*)

grassroots organizations, coupled with the management problems, had an impact—Congress took a forceful role in preventing or slowing many of the proposed changes. CNCS's historical management problems therefore inhibited its ability to hold its grantees responsible, at least in the eyes of Congress.

Similarly, if a network of respected providers performs well, but the government nevertheless decides to change the direction or performance metrics in the contract, it may run into problems. For example, when Indianapolis proposed to change its community center funding mechanism from a fixed amount that increased annually to a model based more on performance, some highly regarded nonprofits and prominent neighborhood residents voiced their opposition to both the city council and the press. These community groups succeeded in modifying the more radical pay-for-performance changes, fashioning a hybrid mixture where most of the centers did not face substantial risks. The city then proceeded more incrementally, dealing with the groups with the worst performance records in hopes of sending a message to other community groups.

Government should always retain the right to set policy, and thus it must enforce accountability. However, network architects must bear in mind that the benefits a well-known nonprofit brings to a government-run network can also prove an impediment if the network manager needs to change policy or impose consequences on such a high-profile participant.

Unintended Consequences

Some governments mistakenly try to shift as much risk as they can—often shifting it to organizations that do not fully understand the scope of the risk. Several Kansas nonprofits unwittingly experienced such imbalanced risk sharing when the state privatized its child welfare system. Kansas transferred nearly all financial and performance risk to nonprofit providers through a managed care model that required providers to deliver all needed services, regardless of cost. On paper the risk transfer made perfect sense.

Contractors could earn a slight profit if they quickly placed children in permanent care. If they failed to do so, they could bear some financial losses. Kansas officials tried to align the economic incentives of the nonprofit contractors with the program goals of the state.

In practice, the risk shifting did not work well. For one thing, mental health costs for the children increased much more than anyone anticipated. Because the partners agreed to provide all needed services, they locked themselves into providing whatever level of mental health care their clients needed. However, neither the government nor the partners anticipated the huge additional costs of providing adequate mental health care for children transitioning into new homes. For another thing, none of the nonprofits previously experienced the pain of dramatically scaling up or down operations in response to winning or losing a contract. As a result, two nonprofits that won multimillion-dollar contracts during the initial 1997 privatization experienced extraordinary difficulties scaling back staff after losing the rebids several years later. Several ultimately proved unable to bear all the financial burdens imposed by the risk-sharing arrangement and were forced to declare bankruptcy. "The nonprofit organizations had little understanding about the risks that they were agreeing to bear for a population that they weren't willing to skimp on," explains University of Kansas professor Barbara Romzek. "The culture of the organizations was such that they couldn't say no to a child who needed extra mental health assistance."

What broader lesson can be gleaned from the Kansas story? Government should think in terms of optimal—not maximum—risk transfer. The public sector cannot walk away from a disaster, because no matter how much risk is theoretically transferred to the private sector, the public is likely to hold the government entity at least partially responsible for any service problems. No black and white lines shape this decision, but a few principles can help.

Risk-Sharing Guidelines

To facilitate successful networked government, the public and private sectors must learn to better share risk. Shifting risk is not free to government, and determining the right approach requires a deep understanding of the roles and capabilities of all network partners.

▲ *Which network partners are best at understanding and managing which risks?* Assigning risk to the organization that best understands and can control the risk maximizes public benefit. Many nonprofit providers, for example, know little about managing financial and performance risk. In these cases, risk should be contracted out to a general contractor or integrator who will accept all of it, or it should be shifted to nonprofits or small business contractors gradually rather than all at once.

▲ *Who is bringing the bulk of innovations to the table?* If nongovernment providers make the case for their services based on their innovations, then they should assume the bulk of the risk.

▲ *How much control does the public sector have over the network and over the particular risk involved?* The less control and authority the public sector retains over processes, the less risk it should assume and vice versa.

▲ *Are the contract costs of the risk shifting worth it?* If it costs the vendors more to accept the risk than the ultimate benefit to the government, then risks should not be shifted.

▲ *Are the risks actually regulatory in nature?* If the potential for future regulatory changes creates project risk, then the government may derive substantial cost benefit by accepting the risk itself.

A good example of once misplaced and now corrected risk shifting in a network response involves economic development in urban areas on real estate parcels with environmental problems, known as brownfields. Environmental concerns always killed the early deals to clean up these brownfields. It was often not the cleanup cost of the site that presented the problems, but rather the risk that after the land came under private ownership, the government would tighten its standards in the future or that improved science would discover new problems. Federal and state officials tried to force private and nonprofit community developers to accept these unknown future risks, but unknown costs exceeded potential benefits by so much that former owners walked away from the property and no new owners surfaced. Eventually cities and states realized they could work with developers to clarify environmental standards, and in some cases indemnify them (after cleanup) against any subsequent liability resulting from conditions that existed prior to the new ownership. Once the risk

Key Risks and Mitigation Strategies

Risk	Mitigation strategy
Failure to perform	Establish dispute resolution mechanisms, service-level agreements and penalties, and contractual "off-ramps" to allow for exit from contract on reasonable grounds.
Termination continuity	Ensure options exist for maintaining the continuity of the operations in the event a partner fails to perform, becomes insolvent, or must leave the project for some other reason.
Transfer of critical skills and knowledge to network	Understand what skills will be performed by the network and retain in-house or third-party consultants with skills and knowledge necessary to monitor the service.
Disruption to operations	Understand and prepare for transition operational challenges. Place responsibility for successful transition on partners.
Inability to scale	Agree on anticipated growth in service demand and plan for capacity and pricing.
Loss of reputation	Ensure that network activities improve both customer satisfaction and the reputation of the government by establishing customer satisfaction incentives at the outset of the relationship.
Cost overruns, time delays	Structure incentives so cost overruns are borne by partner and penalties are assessed for delays.

was understood, private and community developers could help them understand and mitigate the costs.

Benefits of Well-Designed Risk Sharing

As the above example reflects, government can benefit greatly from sharing some risk with the private sector if the risk sharing is well designed. In the United Kingdom, for example, local governments have developed sophisticated risk-sharing and transfer mechanisms for partnerships. In a notably complex public-private partnership, the town of Milton Keynes in southeast England entered into a twelve-year partnership with HBS, a British business services provider, to develop new customer access channels and run all the town's back-office services, including finance, human resources, and administration. The goals of the far-reaching partnership were twofold: modernize and reengineer all the back-office operations without a large upfront investment from the town; and stabilize the town council's operations costs over the twelve-year period. To pay for the $10 million in upfront modernization investments while also making a profit, HBS had to find a way to reduce the number of staff involved in back-office activities by 40 percent—and do so without layoffs.

The complicated structure of the partnership entailed large risks to both parties. Local officials, working with a consultant, wrestled with difficult issues such as what happens to all the physical and intellectual assets if the contract has to be terminated early? Who bears the risk if the partnership ends before achieving the savings from reengineering? What happens if the highly leveraged partner goes bankrupt? Do the employees move back over to government?

A simple principle helped guide council officials in sorting out these complicated issues: the party that is best able to control the risk should bear the risk. HBS, for example, agreed to pay the annual public sector pension payments for city employees transferred to the firm, but the council assumed fund investment performance risk, meaning any annual top-up contributions would still be its responsibility. In a similar vein, if the contract had to be terminated or if HBS could not continue providing service to the council, the costs of getting another provider to step in would be deducted from the HBS payments and the council would have first crack at the assets used to run the operation.

A sophisticated output-based performance regime aligned risks even better by tying HBS's payments to specific service targets. For example, to mitigate the risk that current service levels would suffer during the three-year transition period to the new system, HBS payments were fixed to a basket of indicators, such as invoice payment periods, average time to deal with customer queries, and information system availability, that reflect a rounded view of performance. So if HBS devoted all its time and attention to modernizing the system and neglected current service operations (even the less "critical" services), its payments would fall. Rising service-level targets and a payout to HBS upon completion of the reengineering, in turn, provided strong incentives to complete the modernization on schedule.

It is also possible to share nonfinancial risk, such as the exposure that a public employee faces when exercising discretion in a sensitive area. For example, when a child welfare caseworker moves a child that has been previously abused by a member of her family toward reunification with that family, the caseworker increases the risk of adverse circumstances for herself, the child, and the agency. The caseworker can share reunification risk, however, by soliciting the participation of a respected, community-based partner. The partnership's intervention not only helps government to solve these difficult questions, but also serves as proof to the community that the agency is taking extra due diligence in the case, and such intervention could mitigate damage to the agency if the caseworker's decision leads to an unforeseeable, negative result.

The debate over whether partnering with a respected nonprofit increases or reduces risk to public employees played out vividly when Heidi Brinig, a clinical therapist specializing in child welfare, convinced Rhode Island's Department of Children, Youth, and Families (DCYF) to contract with the Providence Children's Museum. Under this agreement, the museum and its "Families Together" therapists provide an interactive, educational environment in which team members observe and counsel parents and children of court-separated families during supervised visitations. After observations, "Families Together" therapists and DCYF caseworkers jointly formulate recommendations for the family's next steps.

Many state caseworkers initially reacted negatively to the partnership. They worried about sharing any responsibility for the safety of these children with a nonprofit organization. DCYF, after all, remained legally accountable should harm come to any children in the care of the Families Together staff or while DCYF was following their recommendations. The initial lack of trust in Families Together was the foreseeable response of a public agency concerned about avoiding mistakes, but in time the partnership overcame this problem. DCYF caseworkers came to value not only the expert advice offered by Families Together therapists, but they also appreciated their staff's willingness to assume practical responsibilities such as transporting parents and children to and from the visitation site. DCYF also realized that its partnership with Families Together could actually reduce its risk and boost its credibility with the courts and other outside parties by providing better-substantiated arguments for or against reunification. In the end, this enhanced influence afforded DCYF more room to make professional decisions knowing that a respected nonprofit shared in decisionmaking and therefore the risk.

Measuring and Monitoring Performance

Measuring and tracking performance within a complex network is a major challenge for public innovators. The network may need a long time to achieve its outcomes, or a particular agency or entity's contribution to the outcomes may be relatively small, complicating efforts to determine cause and effect. Moreover, even when governments monitor contractors adequately, they often focus solely on inputs, which provide little information about the actual quality of service delivery. "We do a fine job of monitoring contractors. We make sure that they have the number of employees they say they have, that their pencils are sharpened, and that their forms are filled out correctly," says one county social service director. "What we don't do a good job of is evaluating the contractor's *performance*."[17]

Using Technology to Measure Performance

Fortunately, advances in technology have simplified and streamlined the process of collecting performance data, giving governments a clearer picture of how well the overall network and its individual partners perform at any one time. Wisconsin's Department of Workforce Development, for example, uses a data warehouse to collect performance information about each of its contractors. The database provides the state with extensive information about the progress of every welfare-to-work client, which the state uses to analyze whether the contractors are exceeding or falling behind their performance targets.

Arizona's Motor Vehicles Department has also used technological advances to improve data collection and analysis. It established a quality assurance group and audit unit to monitor compliance by third-party providers with the terms of their performance agreements. The assurance group's electronic accountability system centralizes all the data from the third-party companies, tracking everything from the number of transactions a third party does in a given time period, to customer complaint information, to the average amount of time it takes to complete a customer transaction. The system makes it extremely difficult for a provider to defraud the state; it automatically flags those that engage in an unusually high number of transactions, generating an activity report to ensure the work is legitimate.

Until recently, government managers could not monitor the real-time performance of complex, dispersed organizations. But thanks to distributed information technology, networking, and digital record-keeping, service and product providers can now see each other's information immediately; the contract monitor can follow individual cases and aggregate data for online reporting.

For example, advanced performance measures and monitoring tools can improve the quality of child welfare services and the level of employee accountability. Substantial scandals have occurred in many places as states and their agents often lost track of children within the foster care system. Now, using distributed, digital record-keeping tools, agencies can collect relevant information about each child on a daily basis. Through a combination of electronic swipe cards; interactive voice recognition systems; and Internet reporting, the foster parent, school administrator, probation officer, social worker, Medicaid doctor, or counselor can notify a data center of the contacts he has with a child. Caseworkers, whether employed by community-based organizations or the government, can receive daily electronic notifications (even to their smart phones if desired) of all the children in their care. Digital pictures and geographic positioning systems (GPS) systems can enable managers to track whether the caseworker has in fact seen a given child on a given day, and these tools also help managers generate real-time reports of caseworker results. These advances represent a huge improvement over the needle-in-a-haystack task of sorting mountains of paper to obtain clues about employee performance.

Customer Satisfaction Data

The Ohio Bureau of Motor Vehicles uses another important tool for measuring performance—customer satisfaction data—to rate more than 200 private contractors who deliver the state's motor vehicle services. The bureau's information system allows managers to view the monthly customer satisfaction ratings for each provider. This information, together with other performance data, allows the bureau to monitor provider performance closely. Based on this feedback, the bureau terminates the contracts of approximately a half dozen low-performance providers each year.

One Caveat

Network managers should bear in mind that networks may include government partners—often from different agencies—and since networks often depend on market mechanisms to manage resource flows, network rules should apply equally to both internal and external partners.[18] Specifically, internal government service costing should be transparent, and quality and performance standards should apply.

Further, participation in the network should be construed in partnership, not bureaucratic, terms. In Indianapolis, in the 1990s, for example, a distant, slow, and bureaucratic planning department failed to furnish timely and understandable responses, consequently delaying, and sometimes harming, the network of community development partners. These partners did not need city supervision; they required instead a government planner as a team member—albeit one with disproportionate power. Indianapolis was unable to hold the neighborhood partners to performance timetables when the partners' success depended on the responsiveness of a confusing, resistant government agency.

Managing Change

A network's dynamic nature raises difficult questions for its managers and partners. During the life of the network, partners often make discoveries, arrive at new solutions, find existing practices outdated, or prove underlying assumptions inaccurate.[19] How can government managers and partners navigate between the dangers of inflexible, outdated contract terms and their public responsibility to stay true to a fair, competitive structure and their original goals? Standard operating practices—restrictive, long-term contracts locking governments and contractors into goals that could become irrelevant if statutes change or economic conditions shift—often come back to haunt public sector attempts at networked governance.

The very complexity of networked governance ensures that partners will learn better methods and additional facts as the network relationship matures. Thus, even diligent efforts to define performance in a complicated arrangement fail unless they accommodate dynamic change. Often, many initial benchmarks regarding caseloads, service levels, and other metrics are "guesstimates" because public sector accounting and budgeting systems typically capture little of this information.

In many states, child welfare caseloads rose dramatically after highly publicized tragedies about increased child abuse in the home. To avoid a repeat of these incidents, caseworkers more aggressively removed children from their birth homes and placed them in group homes or foster care. The result? Many of the private group home providers became overwhelmed by the increased demand, and the expanded foster care system swept up more marginal foster parents. Social workers monitoring the children could not keep up with the scores of additional children. States rushed to increase their networks of group homes and foster care, paying per diem for care. But this payment system encouraged long stays and little permanency for the child. Only after a significant congressional reform forced states to produce permanent placements within the shortest time appropriate—not to exceed one year—did contracts change to encourage family reunification. The lesson? A network that blindly enforces original contract stipulations despite shifting circumstances restricts the network's potential.

One caution: government networks must weigh the benefits of flexibility against the need to keep partners honest. Too often private partners intentionally bid low—using postcontract "discoveries" to justify contract change orders that convert a loss-leader contract into a profitable one.[20]

Balancing Flexibility and Accountability

Network managers must retain as much flexibility as possible without acquiescing to constant and unwarranted requests for changes in performance targets and standards. Providers need some certainty in order to plan their budgets, hire staff, and ensure continuity of care. Meanwhile, governments cannot measure performance over time if the measures keep changing each year. Balancing these two seemingly contradictory impulses is extremely delicate. Some managers succeed by establishing executive steering committees comprising senior officials from both the government and the private sector to resolve major issues regarding the contracts or networks. Their job: to evaluate strategic objectives and align future services with changing case requirements. These steering committees can also help build stronger relationships between the partners; one partner's discoveries could easily spark improvements in another's process without necessarily mandating a change in government definitions or measurements of performance. A dynamic but fair process occurs more frequently when the original contract pays sufficient attention to the underlying values and clarity about broad goals. With a structure like this established in advance, problems and disagreements become opportunities for improvement. The United Kingdom partnership boards discussed in chapter 5, for example, provide a forum where contractors, government officials, and stakeholders come together to solve problems, resolve conflicts, and discuss contract scope expansions.

Maintaining the dynamic nature of a network implies constant change not only in the relationship between the members of the network, but sometimes even in the very objectives of the endeavor itself. Citizens interact with the network in different ways and at differing points, a situation that produces uneven, or asymmetrical, information, with different members of the network having different pieces of information and perhaps as a result reacting in quite different ways from other network members. One contractor, for example, may see that a certain drug treatment is very unpopular even though the contract monitor, insulated from the clients, may still insist that it be completed. Unless the network has an organized structure to channel these citizen experiences into continuing improvements, asymmetrical information flows will produce tension and distortion instead of innovation. The governance structure of the network, described in the last chapter, should also include periodic access to policymakers and technical experts. Regular meetings to evaluate overall policy and make necessary changes, monthly financial metrics, and a well-trained contract manager who receives continual feedback from the ultimate customers all help ensure that the partnership produces continuous improvement.

Meaningful incentives also help networks manage change effectively. When the Navy built its Navy Marine Corps Intranet, managers had to balance the vendor's need for flexibility with their duty to hold the vendor accountable for key cost and performance goals. NMCI director Rear Admiral Charles Munns and his team came up with a novel approach to balancing the flexibility-accountability tension. Clauses in the contract with NMCI's primary contractor, EDS, were intended to provide generous performance bonuses for high customer satisfaction levels. This process, designed to give the Navy leverage in suggesting customer improvements and EDS financial incentives to fix problems, tested both parties, as EDS commitments far exceeded contract revenues. The example illustrates the need for mechanisms to resolve service-level issues without arduous contract alterations; such mechanisms are crucial to maintaining a network's dynamic nature.

Adaptive Management

A tool called adaptive management furnishes another useful tactic for managing the tension between flexibility and accountability. First adopted in the environmental sector, adaptive management provides partners with flexibility in the goals and the methods they select to achieve them. In this model, progress is measured by continuous feedback and evaluation during the program, instead of by a checklist of performance targets at the program's conclusion. The state of Hawaii's Executive Office on Aging used adaptive management as its accountability tool when it formed a network of public, private, and nonprofit providers to improve end-of-life care for Hawaii's terminally ill and low-income elderly. The initiative, Kokua Mau, enabled elder care and end-of-life providers to share resources for the benefit of clients and their families. The Office on Aging's management model gave network members "permission to change the objectives when the wrong questions have been asked," explains Kokua Mau's program manager Joanne Crocker. By routinely reevaluating performance measures, partners can ask program managers to adjust outcomes to meet more realistic goals and permit individual providers to use money where it is most needed rather than funding efforts in ineffective programming areas.

The Office on Aging maintains focus on a consistent vision and mission but manages vendors as true partners, constantly massaging the metrics. Information gleaned from regular measurement and evaluation of performance indicators and action can either result in program management changes or reinforce existing positive outcomes. For example, program managers noticed that after several months of speeches by members of the hospice speakers' bureau, Kokua Mau had raised awareness of hospice programs and increased the referral rate of clients by 40 percent. Thanks to Kokua Mau's adaptive management model, providers used their discretion to channel more resources into the speakers' bureau because it produced better outcomes than some originally funded activities intended to increase client referrals.

A Portfolio Approach to Relationship Management

Most government agencies see contracts not as relationships but rather as one-off discrete tasks to be carried out by the procurement division with some assistance from the agency in question. Rarely does government consider coordinating and managing the set of relationships as a portfolio. The main components of a good relationship portfolio management program include implementing control systems, minimizing risk of dependency, measuring partner performance, rationalizing the portfolio, and identifying opportunities to reduce costs. An agency that does not use this management approach can end up with often redundant, sometimes conflicting contracts, partnerships, and networks that do not square with the strategic framework that drives the agency's activities.

That was the situation Terri Shaw confronted when she took over as the chief executive of the U.S. Department of Education's Office of Federal Student Aid (FSA). FSA spent more than $450 million a year on technology contracts with a variety of vendors, outsourcing more than 82 percent of the department's budget—little of it coordinated. "We had a vendor here, a vendor there, a vendor here, all on different contract timelines, all on different contract terms, all with different technology platforms, all with different businesses," explained Shaw. "They all had different everything, yet they all needed to exchange data. It made no sense to me."

Shaw was determined to rationalize this chaotic situation. She approached this challenge by first evaluating the entire set of service contracts at FSA in much the same manner a financial planner would do when looking at someone's investment allocations. Shaw also looked at the extent to which each contract aligned at a high level with the strategic goals of the office. This kind of exercise helps organizations evaluate which partner relationships make sense and which do not.

"We layered all the contracts," says Shaw. "The picture was very ugly." The office did not have a larger view of how the vendor contracts did or did not relate to one another. The contracts did not have a controlling common purpose, a failure that resulted in millions of wasted dollars. Shaw found, for example, that FSA paid one provider to collect and process student loan payments while paying others to collect on delinquencies. The fragmentation precluded any incentive to manage the entire life cycle of the loan. As a result, too many loans passed into delinquency and then default.

Shaw knew the department had neither the personnel infrastructure nor the funds to build a new system. She became convinced that a better approach would be to issue a request for proposal where one or more vendors could propose to integrate the multiple contracts and vendors into a single contract. Five separate technology systems operated by multiple vendors were eventually replaced with a single system to handle the office's direct loan servicing functions, loan consolidation processes, and collection activities for the $100 billion in federal student loan obligations.[21] The larger issues of timely payment and delinquency avoidance became the contracted performance criteria, rather than the more narrow criteria used in the separate contracts. The department now can better manage credit risk, using new tools and information to locate students who might need credit counseling before default. Best of all, Shaw estimates that adopting this enterprise approach will save the agency around $100 million a year.

Unfortunately, the strategic approach undertaken by Shaw at FSA is rare. Few organizations—in either the public or private sector—use a portfolio approach to manage their relationships with external partners. A survey of more than 100 FTSE (London Stock Exchange) 500 companies

Benefits of Relationship Portfolio Management

Optimizing the contract portfolio
   Significant potential for cost reduction
   Harmonization of key contractual provisions (such as payment mechanisms)
   Economies of scale
   Refinancing gains released

Organizational design
   Operational improvements
   Support services scaled to meet demand
   Resources freed to focus on frontline service delivery

Improving procurement
   Leveraging full buying potential of government
   Better use of frameworks to increase flexibility and reduce
      procurement costs

Control systems
   Stronger audit and control
   Greater responsiveness of government to changing priorities
   Provides evidence necessary to renegotiate contracts effectively

found that 75 percent of respondents did not have systems in place to measure the success of their most critical external relationships.[22] In the private sector, this practice is beginning to change as the benefits of relationship portfolio management become better understood.

Minimizing Dependency Risk

Much like a portfolio of investments, the principal goal in managing a portfolio of networks and partnerships is to get an overall optimal return while minimizing risk. This means developing a portfolio consistent with the strategic goals of the agency. (For a detailed discussion on mission and strategy, see chapter 4.) The agency, however, must balance the value of the portfolio to the agency against the agency's dependency risk on the portfolio. Dependency risk is the strategic, operational, and financial risk that the organization faces from the portfolio.[23] For example, if an agency's primary strategic goal is to focus on policy, it may wish to outsource all of its noncore functions; however, in doing so, it increases its dependency risk. Should something happen to one of its major contractors, the agency may face significant operational setbacks or financial losses. One way of hedging or mitigating this risk is to diversify supplier relationships so that the agency does not become too dependent on any one relationship. Such an approach allows the agency to substitute relationships or expand existing ones in the portfolio without compromising its strategic goals.

That is what the Department of Energy decided to do with the management of the Los Alamos and Lawrence Livermore nuclear weapons labs and the Lawrence Berkeley National Laboratory. The University of California system had been running the government-owned, contractor-operated labs ever since the early 1940s when the university had participated in the Manhattan Project. But in response to some widely publicized embarrassments in recent years, including continuing security failures, contracts for managing all three labs have been put up for competitive bid for the first time and will be bid in separate contracts. Defense firms, government contractors, nonprofit institutes, and other universities have lined up to compete for the contracts.

Rationalizing the Portfolio

Any successful partnership requires an investment in time and resources, and the return on that investment should be a factor in the decision to enter into a partnership. In investment terms, hurdle rates, or the expected return required to make the investment, are sometimes too low in the public sector. By the same token, exit strategies are not exercised enough; too often government accepts mediocre performance in the belief that replacing a partner creates too much disruption. If a partner's performance does not measure up to standards or it no longer makes strategic sense to continue the partnership, the agency should exercise its option to exit the partnership. To remain consistent with the strategic framework, after regular review the portfolio manager should periodically restructure the portfolio, adding new partnerships and terminating old ones as warranted.

When the United Kingdom's Department of Environment, Food and Rural Affairs undertook such a review, it discovered it had too many partners and too many levels of government involved in service delivery—

much of it overlapping and nearly all of it uncoordinated. "Mapping the relationships caused us to ask several important questions," explains George Trevelyan, a senior manager in the department. "Do we really need this level of complexity in the relationships? Can we reduce the complexity and simplify the networks of relationships?"

This review spurred a complete redesign of the department's rural service system. Funding was discontinued for a large number of organizations whose activities were deemed duplicative or not significant enough to the department's strategic goals.

Although we have tried in this chapter to provide a set of practical guidelines, the truth is that ensuring accountability in a government of networks is more of an art than a science. Achieving success using networks goes far beyond simply enforcing the letter of the contract. It entails knowing when to be flexible and when to be firm; when to shift risk and when to share it; when to add partners to the network and when to shed them.

Success also depends greatly upon choosing the right components of network management in the first place. Without good baseline data, for example, performance targets may be either too ambitious or not sufficiently bold. A government that chooses its partners poorly may not be able to shift any risk to the network. Or if the official uses the wrong integration model, then it may never be possible to get the incentives right.

These are not straightforward black-and-white issues to be addressed by consulting a government procurement manual. Success requires highly skilled and knowledgeable people who can thrive with ample discretion in fast-moving environments. Today it is widely acknowledged by those who follow such things that governments do not have enough of these kinds of men and women. One consequence: the failure of many network approaches. Fixing the "people problem" is the subject of the next chapter.

CHAPTER 6—THE BOTTOM LINE

KEY POINTS

▲ With authority and responsibility parceled out throughout the network, the problem of accountability is one of the most difficult challenges of networked government.

▲ Network architects must define the public good they want to produce, the services and outputs they want to provide, and the goals the network should accomplish. The architects then must determine who should be held accountable for what and by whom. Government expectations must be specific enough to enable the network to deliver services effectively, but without saddling participants with counterproductive and unnecessarily detailed procedures.

▲ Emphasis on important values and clarity of outcomes coupled with flexible processes moves the initiator-participant relationship from an adversarial one to a cooperative, shared-goals perspective.

PITFALLS

▲ Pay that encourages counterproductive conduct, such as cherry-picking the easy cases.

▲ Political support for a nonperforming but respected nonprofit organization.

▲ Shifting risks that produce more costs than benefit.

▲ Bad benchmarking resulting in a financially unsustainable model.

TIPS

▲ Encourage more open information exchange and reduce reliance on costly legal approaches by building greater levels of trust.

▲ Don't suffocate flexibility in a false chase for perfect accountability. Everything, including contracts, should be dynamic, not static, with opportunities for constant learning and adapting.

▲ Provide a method for changing requirements that ensures accountability but also allows for innovation.

▲ Take care to structure base pay and incentives in a way that will lead to the desired outcomes.

EXAMPLES

▲ *Oklahoma Milestones.* Dan O'Brien took over the Community Rehabilitation Services Unit in Oklahoma and immediately noted "twisted incentives." He transformed the financial incentives of the network, moving from paying for activities to buying outcomes. As a result, the network produced more help for workers with disabilities and changed the culture of assistance in the state.

▲ *New Mexico Department of Transportation.* State transportation secretary Peter Rahn wanted more value from the group of companies that construct state roads, so he purchased not just a road but a service: a design, build, and maintenance package that produced a road with a twenty-year warranty.

SEVEN

Building the Capacity for Network Governance

The human capital crisis is also a human capital opportunity. It gives us the opportunity to bring into government people with new skills who think more like businesspeople and to think in a whole new way about what it means to be a government employee.

—Deidre Lee, acquisition director, U.S. Department of Defense

A government manager's job used to be relatively straightforward—you managed a program or service. Although finessing politics, negotiating with unions, and dealing with angry citizens could be trying and difficult, your work and your workforce was largely stable, and the larger your staff and budget, the more prestige you had. You got ahead by advising on policy issues or by excelling at managing government employees. Professionalism meant applying rules in a systematic, standardized, and highly structured manner.

By comparison, managing in a networked government environment demands an entirely different set of competencies and capabilities. In addition to planning, budgeting, staffing, and other traditional government duties, it requires proficiency in a host of other tasks, such as activating, arranging, stabilizing, integrating, and managing a network.[1] To do this, network managers must possess at least some degree of aptitude in negotiation, mediation, risk analysis, trust building, collaboration, and project management. They must have the ability and the inclination to work across sector boundaries and the resourcefulness to overcome all the prickly challenges to governing by network.

Accordingly, commentators often say today's officials need to be more like symphony conductors than drill sergeants. This comparison, however, is a bit simplistic. In actuality, in addition to the conductor, there must be a business manager defining the terms of the engagements and conferring with the musicians, and a marketing person bringing audiences to the performance. To further delve into this analogy, half the orchestra would be employees, while sections like violins would be contracted out, and highly trained musicians would contribute ideas about improving not only their own performance but that of their colleagues.

Yet self-directing, multifaceted, and multiskilled managers are scarce in the public sector. Many government organizations do not have effective contract management capabilities, never mind the far more sophisticated requirements of network management.[2] Building such a capacity requires not only far-reaching training and recruitment strategies, but a full-blown cultural transformation: it requires changing the very definition of "public employee."

The manner in which government delivers programs and services has changed dramatically over the past four decades, but the people the pub-

---

Main Elements of Network Management

✔ Big-picture thinking
✔ Coaching
✔ Mediation
✔ Negotiation
✔ Risk analysis
✔ Contract management
✔ Ability to tackle unconventional problems
✔ Strategic thinking
✔ Interpersonal communications
✔ Project and business management
✔ Team building

TABLE 7-1   Capabilities and Competencies Needed for Network Management

Position	Hierarchical responsibilities	Network governance responsibilities
Chief executive officer, elected official, cabinet officer	Allocate resources Explain to external stakeholders Communicate vision internally and externally	Maximize public value Identify core government values and talents Communicate vision internally and externally
Chief operating officer, director	Protect boss Limit downstream discretion and mistakes	Develop and manage relationships and strategy Understand customer needs (Chief relationship officer)
Manager	Enforce rules Monitor inputs	Manage teams Manage projects and outcomes (Network manager)
Line worker	Follow rules	Solve customer problems
Procurement officer	Prescribe rules Enforce impersonal tight processes	Negotiate Solicit and incorporate best ideas Contract for outside advice
Chief information officer	Direct purchasing, strategy and maintenance of technology	Manage the collection and dissemination of knowledge and information

lic sector recruits, its training programs, and its reward systems have not changed accordingly. People with network skills—collaborative skills not currently highly sought nor valued by government—need to be recruited, rewarded, and promoted. New jobs reflecting those skills must be created and old ones abolished. Likewise, new job descriptions should expect and empower workers to solve problems with increased discretion and fewer layers of supervision (table 7-1).

The Changing Role of the Government CEO

Reshaping the public workforce to fit the imperatives of networked government must start at the top. The leadership responsibilities of a cabinet secretary or agency director or their chief operating officer expand in a network model. From their vantage point, they must assess the public value and, if it is sensible, look "outside their own world" to identify other mechanisms or organizations they can involve to enhance public value.

Keeping the agency's outcome-focused goals foremost—the "product" rather than the "process"—they must fulfill the agency's mission by the best means possible. Talented leaders must understand not only how to address the make-or-buy decision, but how to bring others with needed capabilities and resources into the supply chain.

As an example, consider the plight of a state secretary of health and human services. Whether she realizes it or not, her job is becoming less about running a bureau and more about buying better health and social outcomes—a major and often misunderstood distinction. The management of public employees serves only as a means toward achieving the greater goal of buying these better results. Today's public sector leaders not only need to embrace this mission change from doer to enabler, from rowing to steering, but also must be able to articulate it to public employees and the public at large.[3]

This transition is harder to make than it sounds. In the last round of U.S. military base closures in 1995, for example, most local and federal officials operated inside the formulistic bureaucratic model presented to them: how to give up real estate—bases, for example, and yet protect the numbers of men and women inside their command structures. One leader, Admiral John A. Lockhard, changed the equation. He rejected a simplistic view of consolidation to ask a broader, and at the same time core, question: "What is the best possible way to maximize defense of the country with the dollars available?" This question caused the men and women working for him to change their perspective. Instead of simply trying to figure out whether to transfer government jobs from one place to another, they asked whether a network of public-private partners could take over certain installations and deliver the Navy's work at reduced cost. This broader view resulted in the city of Indianapolis and the Navy together issuing a formal request to the private sector for ideas about how it could use the Naval Air Warfare Center located in the city to continue production of necessary engineering components more efficiently and less expensively. The result: the country's largest base privatization, which knit together public and private resources and contracts, saved millions of dollars, and improved outcomes.

President George W. Bush confronted a similar challenge when he unveiled the USA Freedom Corps, a national service volunteer initiative, during his 2002 State of the Union address. At pivotal points during the last century, American presidents had urged citizens to serve their country and provided a government vehicle for fulfilling these challenges. President Franklin D. Roosevelt started the National Conservation Corps in the 1930s; President Kennedy continued this trend when he created the Peace Corps in the 1960s; President Johnson broadened the theme to include a domestic version of the Peace Corps, Volunteers in Service to America (VISTA); and then in 1990 President Clinton greatly expanded domestic government-supported volunteer service when he created Ameri-Corps and placed it and VISTA under the Corporation for National and Community Service.

The USA Freedom Corps, established by executive order, fundamentally differed from these previous efforts in one important way. It was a coordinating council. Not a program. Not an agency. The president charged USA Freedom Corps not so much to employ young Americans in service as to create a broad network of opportunities for individuals to fulfill the goal of expanding community service across the country. The new organization avoided creating a large government bureaucracy to achieve this goal.

Instead, President Bush drew the attention of the nation and major players in the private and nonprofit worlds to his vision. He put a small White House staff, led by his trusted senior advisor John Bridgeland, in charge of meeting these challenges. The staff did this by building and activating a series of networks—facilitating access to services rather than re-creating services already available. For example, instead of spending millions building and managing a website to encourage volunteerism, USA Freedom Corps provided the digital front door to partners' sites, through which Americans could find information about volunteer opportunities in their own communities.

Most public leaders, as contrasted to their managers, already spend most of their time looking outside the organization. They can leverage these external duties to expand both their knowledge of what others are doing in similar areas and the interest of other groups in partnering with government. As director of the USA Freedom Corps initiative, about two-thirds of Bridgeland's time was spent linking well-connected players in the philanthropic and corporate worlds to produce an extensive network that included foundations, universities, corporate good citizens, school districts, and national associations. His deputy, Ron Christie, brought together various government agencies and departments over which the Freedom Corps had no direct authority and integrated them into a common effort.

Similarly, Wendy Thompson, former chief executive of a city council in the Greater London area, spent 60 percent of her time working with local businesses and nonprofit organizations on partnership and network approaches when she ran the council. Doing so, she told us, was critical to accomplishing most of her top strategic goals from reducing crime to enhancing economic development.

These individuals are the exceptions, however. Executive attention in government still typically focuses on providing political or stakeholder support for existing governmental structures and putting out related fires. Precious little time is spent supervising and fostering partnership arrangements. "In government, the people doing the work of managing the contractors are not the people that really have the skin in the game," says Jack Brock, managing director of sourcing and acquisition issues at the General Accounting Office. Contract management has been pushed down the organization and doesn't get the attention it deserves. Even at agencies such as the Department of Energy and the National Aeronautics and Space Administration, which outsource much of their work, there is a disconnect between senior agency leaders and the contract administrators, says Brock. This needs to change.

To effect change, chief executive officers must also recruit public managers who can thrive in this new environment: people with broad-based, often commercial, backgrounds experienced in managing projects with many moving parts and who can see the larger public value equation—people like Skip Stitt, the former director of enterprise development and deputy mayor of Indianapolis.

Chief Relationship Officer

When he ran the Indianapolis Enterprise Development Unit in the mid-1990s, Skip Stitt oversaw the entire portfolio of relationships the city had developed over the years through dozens of public-private competitions, outsourcings, internal reengineering efforts, and partnerships. At any one time, he might have overseen, directly or indirectly, four dozen or more contracts, as well as a handful of complex public-private networks. He and his small staff controlled nearly every policy and decisionmaking element of the procurement life cycle: evaluation, selection, transition, and contract management.

From this vantage point, Stitt had a broader view of the city's array of third-party relationships than did any of the individual contract managers, allowing him to serve as a reality check on the city agencies managing the contracts. He could provide an informed, objective assessment of which ones worked, which did not, and why. Some of the contracts and relationships that had developed helter-skelter over the years did not make sense from Stitt's enterprise-level perspective. "To do the job right, you have to get out of the historical model of how government is currently put together," explains Stitt. "If you just focus on agencies and service bureaus in the traditional ways, you will miss lots of opportunities to save money and improve service delivery."

As an example, Stitt points to administrative services. Historically every department in the city had its own internal providers or external relationships with couriers; mail houses; microfilm providers; and print, copy, and fax shops. Looking at both the in-house capabilities as well as the contracts holistically, Stitt determined that the city could achieve greater economies of scale—and reduce management headaches—by "joining up" the many city agencies and moving toward a single vendor with expertise in coordinating all the various services. "It was a home run," says Stitt. "We found out that we could consolidate print, copy, fax, and postage services with one provider and save a huge amount of money."

The chief relationship officer also must continually look for opportunities to improve the performance of the organization's multitude of contracts, partnerships, and networks. To meet this challenge, Stitt and his team regularly conducted performance and risk assessments (dubbed initiative management reviews, or IMRs) of city outsourcing and competition projects. The goal was to determine, for any given service, the adequacy of current contract resources, personnel, procedures, and monitoring systems. The review teams also analyzed performance measures and compared them with actual performance. When appropriate they recommended changes in existing measures. One IMR of a three-month-old parking enforcement contract found the contractor's productivity below expectations. Fault could be placed both with the city—for equipment failure and a repair backlog—and with the contractor—for problems in recruitment and training. Soon after the IMR team highlighted the problem, the contractor realized a sharp upturn in productivity.

To help prioritize which projects would be subject to review, Stitt and his IMR team looked at the size of each contract, its potential for problems, the level of complexity of the engagement, and the relative risk of each of the projects. The higher the risk of nonperformance, the higher priority the initiative was given for a review.

Stitt's previous experience before coming to the city made him an effective chief relationship officer. His legal background helped him to get quickly to the heart of a thorny contractual issue, while his commercial experience helped him to understand the nature of complex transactions. Moreover, he had the right personal characteristics for the job: a clear vision of what needed to be accomplished, deep knowledge of what was going on at the street level, good judgment about when to be flexible and when to be demanding, and strong persuasion and collaboration skills.

The Network Manager

Too often agencies shunt contract or network management over to the procurement shop. In a networked environment, contract and relationship management often amount to program management—not something separate that can be offloaded to a different department. Officials should decide where contract management should be located based on the centrality of the work to the agency's mission, not whether contractors or government employees do the actual work. Of course, networks may be supported by other government agencies, but rather than lump all contracts in a single shop for supervision, agencies should assign oversight to the individuals most involved with the applicable mission. Those network assignments need a "manager," not just a contract monitor.

The network manager supervises the day-to-day network activities. Anyone in this position will likely spend a lot more time down in the weeds than will the chief relationship officer. To succeed, however, the network manager must look beyond a narrow set of prerequisites. He must explicitly understand the government's big picture.

Managing a network model also requires attitudes and behaviors not commonly developed as part of the typical public manager's experience. Many public managers, accustomed to exercising hierarchical control over divisions of employees, may be uncomfortable with the more indirect and negotiated control exercised in a network. Others will be unfamiliar with how to come to grips with the continuous change so characteristic of networks. Managing within this environment requires flexibility and adaptability, knowing when to listen and when to lead, and understanding the need for change and flexibility while still managing for high levels of performance against an agreed-upon metric. None of this is easy. It demands a combination of tacit knowledge and strong bridge-building and boundary-spanning skills. The network manager must manage partnership relationships, formulate feedback loops to get results, and monitor performance across both the public and private sectors—all at the same time. The numerous potential minefields involved mean that even the best recruits might not excel at this job for several years.

These new managers must handle the difficult tasks of approving or rejecting the changes to the contract that inevitably arise in outsourcing deals. Some vendors will try to take advantage of government through lowball bids and the subsequent change-order process. Good managers will not let that happen; they know how and when to stand up to their private partners. "If a partner is not performing, you're going to have to deal with their management," explains a Department of Defense official. "You better have a person who has the savvy to do this well."

Given the challenges, what kind of people make good network managers? In our experience, they tend to have a certain set of qualities. They are very organized. They have strong oral communications skills. They think creatively, rather than from the framework of "that's the way we've always done it." They are highly adept at resolving problems. And they know how to create win-win situations.

Often government assigns the job of network manager to a person previously involved in running the service or program when it was done in-house. This approach occasionally works splendidly. After all, these individuals can use their strong knowledge of the service to help the providers succeed. But, unfortunately, these cases are the exception. "Our personal batting average with using incumbents to oversee the new providers was low," explains Stitt. "We typically had better results when we moved in employees from other areas." The reason is simple: some incumbents may not want the partner to succeed, believing, usually mistakenly, that a failed partnership is the best way to get their old job back. Others will try to impose their own sense of best practices, suffocating the reason for the network itself.

In any case, the network managers should be experienced people who act fairly and firmly, attracting the respect of the private partners. The closer the communications between the relationship manager and her private counterpart, the faster problems get resolved, to the benefit of both partners and toward the fulfillment of the agency's mission. Optimally, government executives should be aligned with the partners' executives in project-based teams. Some local governments in the United Kingdom have gone so far as to include their strategic partners on the council's corporate management team.[4]

Well-regarded public officials manage by walking around not only their own shops but those of their partners. They stay alert to both the weak links and the strengths in the network on all sides. As the Navy turned over the operations of the Naval Air Warfare Center in Indianapolis to Hughes Corporation (subsequently Raytheon), longtime government workers, many of whom as program managers monitored vendor contracts, now found themselves on the other side of the line as private employees. What was their primary complaint? These committed workers did not complain about the private ownership; rather they railed against their new government contract managers, who found the time to enforce counterproductive contractual details but not the time necessary to visit the facility.

The Procurement Officer

Traditionally, the most important requirement for a procurement officer to succeed was to know all the rules and follow them without deviation. Not anymore. Acquisition officers must be more than mere purchasers or process managers. A strong knowledge of rules and processes no longer suffices. Procurement officials need to approach their work as a search for the right mix of components, harvesting ideas from key players inside and outside government and making judgment calls every day in a constant effort to improve the situation. "The old days of the stereotypical government acquisition worker are at an end," says Joseph Johnson, director for administration and services at the Defense Acquisition University, the department's training institute. "The worker of the future cannot be just rule bound. Acquisition is no longer about managing supplies; it's about managing suppliers."

To prepare the military's 132,000 acquisition workers for this new environment, the Defense Acquisition University has thoroughly revamped its training curriculum. One important change: getting the acquisition workers to understand that the traditional adversarial, arm's-length relationship that procurement officers have had with their contractors simply will not work anymore. It produces too much confusion and misunderstanding and makes it hard to build the trust needed for partnerships to work over time. To fix these problems the acquisition university embeds contractor representatives into many of the training courses. Contractors regularly participate in classroom discussions, and defense procurement officers act the role of contractors in role-playing exercises. The goal is to help the procurement officers understand the other side better. "If you've worked your entire life as a government procurement officer, it's difficult to write a really good procurement; you don't really understand what's possible for the private sector to do," explains Johnson. "In our courses, they learn that the contractor can go broke. It seems like common sense, but it's something that many contract officers might not have really considered before."

Some agencies aggravate their problems by using the procurement shop as a dumping ground for employees who did not do well elsewhere. The role of procurement officer needs to be elevated within the government food chain. "Being a smart buyer means being able to outthink the companies," says Liam Sarsfield, the deputy chief engineer at NASA. Talented young people need to be recruited into the profession. One positive step: several federal agencies, among them the Department of Treasury, NASA, and the Department of Energy, have created prestigious contracting internship programs to attract a steady pipeline of the best and brightest from the nation's universities.

The New Governance Public Employee

Over the last forty years, the number of line-level U.S. federal employees shrank, while the number of high-level workers remained the same or grew. By 1997, for the first time in history, federal employees at the middle level of government outnumbered those at the line levels (638,427 to 594,126).[5] Brookings Institution scholar Paul Light cites this statistic as an example of the "thickening" of the federal government as it accumulates more and more layers between cabinet secretaries and the FBI agents, customs control officers, food inspectors, and other line-level workers actually delivering services. The thickening phenomenon also follows, however, from the movement toward third-party service provision. A government that relies less on public employees to deliver services and more on private contractors will tend to have fewer low-level workers and proportionately more skilled professionals than one that engages in more direct service provision, as Donald Kettl explains in *The Global Management Revolution*.[6] Similar trends can be observed in private industry. Management guru Peter Drucker argues that "companies will eventually outsource all functions that don't have a career ladder up to senior management."[7]

An Evolving Role

Given these trends, what is the evolving role for the average public employee in a government that increasingly uses networks to fulfill policy goals? Some employees will be asked to make the transition from rowing to steering, from line-level work to vendor management. For many, this shift will not be easy, and for some it will be impossible. In the social services arena, for example, as more and more welfare and child welfare services have been outsourced to networks of private providers, many social workers have been reclassified as contract monitors. Often, these workers fail at their new jobs. Managing contracts takes an entirely different mindset and set of skills than working with an out-of-work parent—skills not typically learned in schools of social work. In Kansas many of the social workers simply could not mentally make the shift, instead reverting to what they knew best: case management. Because the state had already contracted this responsibility to nonprofit organizations, often using different procedures than those formerly used by the state, serious tensions surfaced on both sides as providers complained of micromanagement. But as the discussion of Oklahoma Milestones in chapter 6 showed, there is great opportunity for government professionals open to new ideas to engage in skilled contract management.

Another solution to this problem is better training. After contracting out welfare and child welfare services, Langlade County, Wisconsin, entered into a partnership with universities in the region to provide training in contract management to county social workers. The social workers received classroom instruction and hands-on training in everything from writing good performance objectives to holding outside providers accountable for performance.

Even with the best training, however, some employees will be unable or unwilling to make the transition from doing the work themselves to ensuring that it gets done. In the long run, it is hard to see much of a role for such individuals in the new environment. At the core of governing by network is the proposition that information and knowledge broadly shared can lead to better results. Workers at all levels of government should be "knowledge workers," finding problems and linking them to the source of solutions instead of trying to fix everything in a vacuum. As technology replaces the most mundane low-level functions in government, employees wedded to the old approach in which they contribute most by carefully controlling data and releasing them only as necessary unknowingly subvert their own jobs in an environment where big-picture thinking, flexible approaches, and knowledge sharing as a means of problem solving dominate. Conversely, the government employees who will excel are those who manage for results instead of processes, use technology and networks to troubleshoot, and see their agencies as a means to an end—the mission—instead of an end in itself. One type of individual, in particular, we believe is likely to thrive in a networked government environment: "connectors."

Connectors

In his best-selling book *The Tipping Point,* Malcolm Gladwell introduced the concept of the "connector." These individuals effortlessly span several very different worlds, bringing people together from these disparate environments. In a networked world, governments need more connectors—people whose background and temperament enable them to build up a trove of relationships across the public, private, and nonprofit sectors and leverage these relationships to build networks of mutual benefit. Good connectors look outside a narrow box to help identify who should be brought to the table and how the sum of the parts could exceed the whole.

Hank Helton is one of Gladwell's connectors. He has spent his entire career building collaborations between public, private, and nonprofit organizations, first as one of the principals of a community development corporation called Southeast Community Capital, then as head of Nashville's Office of Affordable Housing. Southeast Community Capital acts as a venture capitalist of sorts for nonprofit organizations and for-profit businesses trying to breathe life into economically depressed areas in states like Tennessee, Kentucky, and West Virginia. Helton learned early on in his job that he could not succeed without building a cross-sector network of relationships. "In order to penetrate the market and leverage dollars, we had to develop a series of strategic partnerships," Helton relates. He would partner with just about anyone who could foster growth in depressed local economies—mayors, state and regional economic development agencies, local chambers of commerce, developers, contractors, bank officers, and the like. Much of his success relied on his ability to draw on these relationships to bring people from different business environments together and act for mutual benefit.

When he took the job with the city of Nashville, he used the skills and contacts he developed in the private sector to pull together people from all walks of life—realtors, affordable housing advocates, banks, public housing agencies, developers, community development corporations, and other organizations—in an effort to produce more affordable housing in the city. Helton understood that configuring a cross-sector solution also depends in large part on having an appreciation of the assets of others. By knowing how to operate flexibly across enterprises, he is able to gather the knowledge necessary to trigger the necessary connections. As government moves more and more to a networked model, effective governance will depend on attracting more individuals like Helton—people who come from team-based, project-oriented environments and who listen well, lead by example, and understand the big picture. People who come from overly bureaucratic environments with highly developed hierarchical and autocratic skills in their day-to-day supervision of employees will typically not add nearly as much value through connections or the broad vision that triggers them.

A good connector, however, does not necessarily have to come from the private sector. Lisa Gregorio proved this when she was charged with forming hundreds of local Citizen Corps homeland defense councils for USA Freedom Corps and given only months to do it. A twenty-year veteran of the Federal Emergency Management Agency, Gregorio had also previously worked at the state, local, and regional levels of government. Thanks to this background, she knew hundreds of players across the country in the emergency planning community. Her existing networks helped her to identify and bring together the right people to build the Citizen Corps network. Within two years, she helped create more than 1,000 Citizen Corps councils across the country.

Meanwhile her previous experience in state and local government made her sensitive to the fact that every community differed; she knew that trying to impose a one-size-fits-all federal solution on them would not work. "We did not prescribe a right or wrong process for states and local governments," says Gregorio. "We said here's the mission, here's what we want you to accomplish, but how you get there is up to you."

Getting from Here to There

Neither the jobs we describe in this chapter nor people with the skills to fill them exist in sufficient numbers in most governments today. In fact, most government agencies are still a far cry from the vision outlined in this chapter. Government reforms over the last fifty years have worked assiduously to "professionalize" (that is, specialize) work and tightly manage information. Effective network governance requires more public employees with a broad knowledge of processes and organizations and a deep appreciation of the importance of open information to a continuously learning organization. These skills, the skills required to succeed in a networked economy and government, are quite sophisticated. Explains Harvard University professor John Donahue: "The kinds of skills involved in orchestrating a high degree of collaboration between the public and private sectors are very high-level skills. They're similar to those needed to be an investment banker, a venture capitalist, or senior-level consultant. They don't come cheap."

Yet while governing by network demands more skilled people at the higher levels of government, the gap between the opportunities outside and inside government for individuals with these skills grows daily. As Brookings' Paul Light shows in *The New Public Service*, the public sector generally does not attract enough top talent.[8] To fix this, government personnel systems need to transform the way they recruit, train, and reward employees, and job descriptions and policies must allow change to happen.

Recruitment

Lynn Scarlett found all this out after being named assistant secretary of the Department of the Interior in 2001. Scarlett came to the federal government from the policy world, where she had been president of the Reason Foundation, a public policy think tank that has produced dozens of studies and books on government contracting and public-private partnerships.[9] Her experience at Reason prepared her intellectually for the human capital challenges she faced in government, but even she was surprised at the dearth of capacity in the areas of contract and network management. Her department simply did not have enough people with strong business and transaction backgrounds. Explains Scarlett: "When we'd sit down at the negotiations table with concessionaires and contractors, there wasn't equal knowledge. We had to bring in a consulting firm to just help us even the playing field. Most of our staffing was scientists, ecologists—people with knowledge of the lands and water. We had little business and management capability."

With the Department of Interior increasingly reliant on partnerships to run its operations and meet its policy goals, Scarlett felt that the capacity gap could result in failed partnerships. In response, Scarlett and her staff created a strategic human capital plan outlining the new skill sets they needed in the department and formulated a plan for getting them. One thing was obvious from the beginning: they needed more people with a collaborative mind-set. "We used to have an inward-looking culture," said Scarlett. "We needed people who don't think in an insular fashion." Recruiters and human resource departments were told to look for people with skills in conservation, communication, collaboration, and cooperation—what Interior calls the four Cs. This led the National Park Service, for example, to search for more managers and leaders who were better integrated into the community in which the individual parks reside.

The Department of Interior also introduced a creative recruitment initiative that brought about an internship program in financial management. The department employed students seeking master's degrees in business administration as summer interns, asking them to create business plans for the individual national parks. These business students helped park managers think more creatively about how to meet rising demands at a time when resources were fixed or declining. One intern was Pat Madden. In the late 1990s he spent a summer working on a business plan for Port Reyes, a part of the Golden Gate National Recreational Area. After graduation he passed up a much larger salary from an investment bank and instead returned to Port Reyes to help with business operations. Within just a few years, the whiz kid was promoted to budget chief of the entire recreational area. In this position, he has used his business skills to assist Superintendent Brian O'Neill (who was introduced in chapter one) in expanding the park's facility-based public-private partnerships and leveraging private funding for public investments.

Another model for attracting new governance skill sets comes from Great Britain. In the mid-1990s the central government created an organization called "Partnerships UK" as part of a broader effort to improve government's capacity to conduct public-private partnerships. Partnerships UK tries to help agencies become smarter purchasers of services by standardizing contracts and specifications, providing help-desk support, highlighting best practices, and rotating employees in and out of agencies for up to six months at a time. Partnerships UK employees come from rich and varied backgrounds; they are investment bankers, lawyers, management consultants, and engineers. All of them have commercial experience in delivering projects, thereby filling a major capacity void in the central government. "The civil service career strategy doesn't lend itself to developing commercial deal capabilities," says Helen Dell of Partnerships UK. "Civil servants aren't recruited in for those skills."

In a similar vein, the Dutch government recognized that its expanded use of partnership approaches constituted a major change for civil servants. To help them in the transition, the government created a Public-Private Partnership Center within its Ministry of Finance to act as a clearinghouse of sorts for the government on public-private partnership (PPP) issues. Like Partnerships UK, the center publishes best-practice reports, issues guidelines and advises agencies on individual projects ranging from schools to high speed railways. In addition, nearly every major Dutch government department has its own PPP unit that focuses on developing and overseeing individual PPP projects.

Reforming Civil Service

The United Kingdom revamped its civil service curriculum to better meet the training needs of today's public managers. One goal is to provide civil servants with more training in forming and managing complex partnerships to benefit the public. The civil service courses now include a greater emphasis on networked government skills, such as managing contracts, being smart buyers, working in partnerships, and developing business management skills.

In a similar vein, the Pentagon's Defense Acquisition University, which was profiled above, also offers week-long executive training sessions in acquisition strategy for generals, admirals, and other military brass whose primary responsibilities do not necessarily include direct oversight over procurement. The courses have been so successful that NASA is now requiring all its senior project managers to attend at least one of them.

While such efforts are to be applauded, the fact remains that at a more fundamental level, today's civil service systems are in many ways incompatible with the movement to networked government. As Donald Kettl notes, "Managing indirect government requires skills that the traditional civil service system tends to either undervalue or ignore."[10] Most civil service promotion and retirement systems, for example, heavily favor those who spend their entire careers in government. As we argued earlier, it is harder for people who have never been in the private sector to understand fully the needs and motivations of their network partners.

Government needs more employment opportunities, and more career paths, that allow managers to move more easily between the public, private, and nonprofit sectors and to take on projects for discrete periods of time. Revolving door statutes and job classification systems currently discourage these placements. To be sure, some controls are needed on government officials cashing out and using their clout and contacts in government to secure work for their new employer, but a better balance needs to be found than exists today. Government needs more, not fewer, people who have worked for the private sector. Individuals with experience working for contractors may be more effective negotiators on behalf of taxpayers. Why? Their experience enables them to better understand when a provider might agree to a lower price or higher output or, conversely, when government is making needless demands. There is simply no better way to understand the capabilities and pressures of third-party providers than through on-the-job training. For example, one interesting exception to the current restrictions involves "rotational assignments" offered by NASA and the Department of Energy—programs that allow employees to spend months at a time with private contractors.[11]

Other encouraging developments are occurring at the state level; Florida and Georgia, for example, have fundamentally restructured their civil service systems to provide more flexibility for people to move in and out of government, among other things. Meanwhile at the federal level, agencies such as the Department of Homeland Security, the Federal Aviation Administration, the General Accounting Office, and the Internal Revenue Service have been allowed to replace the standard federal civil service system with alternative employment systems that allow more flexibility and accountability. And there have been similar efforts in the United Kingdom, Australia, and New Zealand. Such efforts toward increased flexibility in public sector personnel systems will give public leaders greater freedom to shape a workforce more aligned with a networked model of government. But the reform efforts face a more fundamental incongruity: a network forms around a problem, solves it, and then allows many of those involved to move on to the next problem. This is not the way governments are currently organized. Government human resource systems place a high value on protecting careers and encouraging development of specialized skills. Few incentives exist to detour from this path to work on collaborative programs; such detours simply mean giving more credit to some other agency or organization. This mind-set needs to change because the capability to coalesce temporarily around a problem, solve it, and then move to the next problem is critically important for the new governance.

In a government long on very specialized skills and short on customer-centric problem-solving capabilities, public employees will often need to come together across governmental barriers and with the other sectors to craft a solution to a public policy problem. Increasingly government requires these cross-agency, cross-sector project teams for many issues, whether constructing a road that affects environmental and business interests, building a new weapons system, or fixing the small signs of social and property decay—what author George Kelling has termed the broken windows[12]—necessary for successful community policing. Public-sector personnel systems, and career incentives should not only allow employees the mobility necessary to form these project teams—both to initiate and sometimes to manage the network—but also give considerable weight to participation in successful collaborative projects for career advancement.

Education and Training

The gap between the skill sets needed to govern the networked state and those that currently exist could be closed by more attention from graduate schools of public administration and public policy. According to many experts, the curriculum at many of these schools has been slow to keep up with the movement to network service provision.[13] Most programs focus on policy, economics, or management of more traditional hierarchical public organizations. A graduate student interested in contract or network management will likely find more options in the business school. When collaborative governance is taught, the focus often centers on political issues rather than on management issues.[14]

These divisions between most business schools and schools of government represent part of the problem. The core of the management innovations Indianapolis adapted, for example, when it began its public-private competition program in the early 1990s came from the Harvard Business

School. Public policy and administration programs need to offer courses on negotiation, project management, contract writing, network management, and cross-sector governance. For example, a new initiative at Harvard's John F. Kennedy School of Government, the Weil Program on Collaborative Governance, is designed to train students and develop research around the different sets of skills necessary for network management. Public policy schools are uniquely situated to help fill the critical need for more people in government with sophisticated business management skills by reaching out to their business school counterparts or developing collaborative governance programs. The availability of more such programs would go a long way toward preparing tomorrow's future public sector leaders for the changing shape of government they will encounter when they enter the public sector.

Why Does Any of This Matter?

Governments will suffer consequences from the failure to update government human capital systems to reflect the new shape of government. According to the conventional wisdom, governments lacking strong third-party management and monitoring capabilities will be vulnerable to voracious contractors who will seek them out for profit and pillage. This caricature bears little resemblance to reality. To be sure, contractors will pursue their self-interest. But in the long run their self-interest lies in partnering not with weak, pushover government agencies but with the smartest, toughest, most sophisticated governments. "Wise firms, nonprofits, or agencies will always seek out the most capable contract partners," writes University of Vermont professor Phillip Cooper. "It may be possible to get an advantage over a weaker partner in regard to costs or work on the front end, but over the long term weak partners produce problems that carry costs."[15]

The cases we studied bear this out. On several occasions firms declined to enter into lucrative contracts when they believed weak management capabilities on the government-client side presented unacceptably high risks of failure. The incremental dollars simply did not justify the risk to their brand and reputation that comes with a bad engagement. These examples reflect the critical fact that strong commissioning capabilities not only deter bad providers, but also attract good ones.

CHAPTER 7—THE BOTTOM LINE

KEY POINTS

▲ Government needs people with new network skills—collaborative skills currently neither highly sought nor valued by government. Building such a capacity requires not only far-reaching training and recruitment strategies, but a full-blown cultural transformation: it requires changing the very definition of "public employee."

▲ While governing by network demands more skilled people at the higher levels of government, the gap between the opportunities outside government and inside government for these kinds of individuals grows daily.

PITFALLS

▲ Leaders who confuse the forest and the trees, mistaking activities such as paying for Medicare with that of achieving actual public value such as improving health.

▲ Human resource systems that further the tree problem by recruiting and promoting people into narrow jobs.

▲ Too many employees with narrow vision caused by too many years of specialized skill development without access to a broad array of outside thinking.

TIPS

▲ Contract managers should become network managers and walk around not only their own shops but those of the vendors.

▲ Recruit some connectors with new skills and lots of (ethical) relationships.

▲ Overhaul civil service laws and procedures to provide the flexibility required to meet the human capital needs of government by network.

EXAMPLES

▲ *Department of Defense Acquisition University*. The Pentagon has thoroughly revamped its acquisition training curriculum. One important change: getting Defense employees to understand that the traditional, adversarial, arm's-length relationship that procurement officers have had with their contractors simply does not work anymore. Another innovation: week-long executive sessions on acquisition strategy for generals, admirals, and their private sector counterparts.

▲ *The United Kingdom's Civil Service College*. The United Kingdom has begun to offer civil servants more training in forming and managing complex partnerships. Civil service courses now include a greater emphasis on networked government skills, such as managing contracts, being smart buyers, working in partnerships, and developing business management skills.

EIGHT

The Road Ahead

The study of networks is not new. By now most readers have heard that by virtue of their own personal networks they are only six degrees of separation away from each of their fellow citizens. Most office workers have complained about their computer networks going down because someone else on the network managed to crash the entire system.

In short, as more than one writer has noted, we now live in the "Age of the Network," and there is no shortage of effort to decipher this development and explain what it means to our economy and society.[1] Go to Amazon.com and you will find slews of books with titles like *The Differentiated Network, The Living Network, Networks and Netwar,* and so on. There are books about computer networks, biological networks, communications networks, and terror networks. Scores of academics have made a cottage industry out of studying the science, the mathematics, and the sociology of networks. Yet we appeal here to public innovators: government officials dedicated to squeezing every possible ounce of public value out of available resources. To them we suggest that governing by network can produce substantial benefits.

Significant changes in our society both enable governing by networks and require it. The problems that citizens and their elected representatives face today are too complex for a one-size-fits-all solution administered by a hierarchical bureaucracy. Citizens who routinely benefit from highly individualized responses in the commercial world are less and less likely to tolerate a government that insists on delivering uniform services. Meanwhile technological advances can increasingly decentralize and customize public services by allowing a network manager to coordinate the actions of numerous partners in real time. Our complex society both demands a new public sector governance and delivery model and provides the tools for innovators to respond to those demands. We conclude this book with a few broad principles for public innovators to keep in mind as they embark down the path of governing by network.

Focus Less on Programs and More on Public Value

More often than not, when a concerned elected official sees a problem in her constituency, she tells a staffer to solve it. This approach typically works for simple, compartmentalized, ad hoc issues. But in more complex matters, especially where the observed problem points to a systemic weakness, this perfectly rational action can produce three unfortunate side effects. First, the government official receiving the assignment typically thinks largely in terms of her own programs and authority, thus limiting the available options. Second, the approach produces a mechanical response that often misses the big picture. Third, it often presupposes a government answer, resulting in a greater use of tax dollars than might have been necessary if a more expansive view had been taken.

When the problem involves a larger public policy issue, we would urge officials to first determine what important public outcome they want to

Principles for Governing by Network

✔ Focus less on programs and more on public value
✔ Don't get lost in the fine print
✔ Money is *a* tool, not *the* tool, for forming networks
✔ The perfect is the enemy of the good
✔ Develop a new set of core competencies
✔ Downsize and upsize simultaneously

produce and then to address how best to solve it. Framed in this way, the best answer will less likely be a government-only solution. A monopolistic governmental agency, after all, is unlikely to be the best in class for all aspects of a particular response. Instead, by explicitly focusing on maximizing public value, the range of potential solutions typically widens to include the private and nonprofit sectors as well as other levels of government. This in turn allows public officials to explore more fully important issues such as:

▲ How to leverage private dollars
▲ How to construct solutions that knit together partners from all sectors and often multiple levels of government
▲ Where to look outside government for access to specialized expertise, cutting-edge technology, and top-notch management talent

A greater focus on public value also will gradually change the way government is conceptualized; the idea of government based on programs and agencies will give way to government based on goals and networks. Instead of seeing their jobs mostly as managing public employees, public executives will view their role as working out how to add maximum public value by deploying and orchestrating a network of assets.

Getting to this point will not be easy. One daunting obstacle, for example, is the legislative branch. By dint of the very way legislative committees are organized, many legislators will find it uncomfortable when the network stretches across the authority of more than one committee. Reformers, therefore, must make the benefits of the network more clearly tangible to legislators. Lining up outside support can help. Neighborhood groups, for example, that normally might not notice the benefits of a networked approach until well after a bill is voted on, but who might be enthusiastic supporters if they understood the significance, can be powerful allies.

Second, reformers should advocate to the legislature the public value produced by the network, not the network itself. Indianapolis did not ask its city council to authorize the country's first large-scale wastewater privatization, but offered instead a plan to eliminate a proposed 30 percent increase in water rates by hiring outside providers.

Finally, when a government leader intends to present several new large-scale approaches to different issues, it may be prudent to encourage legislators to submit the approaches to a committee with broad-based juris-diction, somewhat akin to the base-closing model. This way the legislature can truly weigh the broader costs and benefits, instead of simply focusing on whether a specific agency's ox is getting gored. Another approach is to have an authorized commission submit all of the suggestions for change as a package, which must be voted up or down in its entirety.

Don't Get Lost in the Fine Print

A networked approach should continually produce new ideas and new ways of doing things. Successful networks often individualize their responses to citizens with differing problems. Each of the participating partners pro-vides an opportunity for learning that can enhance the overall quality of the service. Incorporating these experiences into the solution requires a high level of flexibility, a certain amount of creativity, and a dynamic gov-ernance structure. Government procurement rules, however, are designed to ensure an honest system, not encourage innovation. Procurement offi-cers and contract managers generally display great attention to detail, but are not known for their creativity. This creates problems because the net-work needs to be managed around key values and performance objectives, not simply by the fine print of the contract. Translating the mission of the network into a set of common and understood values will help both the network manager and the parties to produce more value per public dol-lar, provide a framework for true partnership, and safeguard against the network becoming static, outdated, or even obsolete.

This does not mean that government should ignore the details in the contract. It simply means that officials should interpret them in the spirit of the agreed-upon values and outcomes, recognizing that if their applica-tion creates counterproductive results, they need to be renegotiated, not ignored. Moreover, even while networks allow enormous elasticity with respect to the way services are configured and delivered, government inno-vators must ensure that all partners observe basic rules and guarantee val-ues inherent in a public system. The progressive administrator will preserve the best of what bureaucracies offer and discard the worst, phasing out the enforcement of counterproductive input rules, while strengthening quality and equity enforcement.

Money Is *a* Tool, Not *the* Tool, for Forming Networks

Government can create a network by requesting proposals asking for a networked solution and backing it with contractual money. This direct route will more likely than not produce a response reasonably close to that envisioned, albeit limited by the prescriptive terms that generally accompany requests for proposals. Often this will be the best approach to meet the desired goals of policymakers, but not always. Because one purpose of networks is to provide creative and flexible answers to complex problems, a tightly worded RFP may unnecessarily constrict public value.

Besides money, public leaders have an entire tool kit of assets they can draw on to bring together partners. Sometimes they can connect partners by filling a gap in capacity or infrastructure. For example, a city could provide the information technology expertise and support that allows many interested groups to coordinate their solutions more closely. Or the mayor or governor might use the bully pulpit or her convening authority to articulate the need for a networked response to a major city problem such as teen pregnancy or literacy. On a more mundane level the glue for putting a network together may simply consist of an innovative public leader creating his own civic switchboard by connecting parties to each other that have complimentary programs or services.

Authority is another asset. Officials can "loan" their authority to an integrator; for example, by making a community development corporation eligible for special grants. Or a judge might partner with a network of service providers whose control over individuals is enhanced by potential sanctions from the court.

The Perfect Is the Enemy of the Good

No matter how well designed the network might be, or how many rules are correctly followed, over time one problem or another will surely arise. Unforeseen circumstances will occur. New technologies may render original technical specifications obsolete. Additional partners may need to be added—or some subtracted. And while some performance indicators may go up, others may go down. After all, measuring performance ensures that government will likely get more of what it measures but sometimes in unanticipated ways. Thus flexibility and adaptation become a performance measure as well, and their importance dictates a need for a bendable structure that can embrace change.

Take the Coast Guard's deepwater project that we discussed in chapter 4. Not surprisingly, the events of September 11, 2001, raised questions about some of the original goals and targets of the program. A RAND Corporation study determined that because of the enhanced terrorist threat, two-thirds more cutters and a larger number of aircraft were needed than originally recommended. This does not mean that the Coast Guard's innovative procurement approach failed. Instead, like many previous examples cited throughout this book, it points to the importance of building in mechanisms that permit changes to be made in midstream.

The privatization debate offers some useful lessons. Few proponents suggest that privatization will uniformly produce success. And surely, although it is not always mentioned, few opponents argue that government bureaucracies are uniformly effective.[2] Rather, the question is which delivery system in a particular instance is most likely to produce the greatest public value. The goal is not to build a perfect system, but to make meaningful enhancements over the status quo.

Develop a New Set of Core Competencies

As more and more agencies forge partnerships with third parties, agency performance will largely depend on how well the partnerships are managed. To achieve high performance in this environment, governments will need to develop core capabilities in a host of areas where today they have scant expertise. Three of the most important of these capabilities are conceptualizing the network, integrating it, and developing effective knowledge-sharing practices across the network.

Conceptualizing a network requires senior public officials who can see through restrictive government walls into relationships that might produce value and ask the basic questions—often overlooked in government: what results are to be produced, who should perform the necessary activities, where should they be performed, and in what sequence. As business guru Michael Hammer writes, innovation requires leaders who are prepared to defy "conventional assumptions about how work should be done . . . and [eliminate] the assumption that interferes with a strategic goal."[3] Knowing to ask these questions, let alone figuring out the answers, requires a different set of skills than those typically valued in existing governmental systems.

Designing the network is difficult enough, but managing it presents its own challenges. We devoted a relatively large portion of this book to the subject of integration because we believe that having the capacity to integrate networks lies at the very heart of networked governance. Unfortunately, most public agencies lack this skill set. This needs to change. In a networked environment, knowing how to integrate partners effectively needs to become a core competency of government, particularly in agencies that do most of their work through partners.

This does not mean that governments should discontinue using private and nonprofit organizations to integrate public-private networks and always try to be their own integrator. For the many reasons discussed earlier in the book, most government agencies cannot become as skilled at integration as world-class organizations specializing in this work. Governments should, however, at least know enough about it to effectively manage private sector integrators and step in and supervise the network themselves if something goes terribly wrong.

Third, governments need to develop much stronger competencies in sharing knowledge. Today the difference between success and failure often rests on how well the parts of the network communicate and share knowledge at multiple points and in various ways. Knowledge sharing transcends mere mechanical or technical matters: it is the very heart of the network. Enormous value is derived from the disparate experiences of many points of citizen contact that are translated into useful responses by the many partners involved in the network, allowing each to adjust its responses appropriately.[4]

Cross-organization and cross-sector knowledge sharing are still in their formative years. Even the private sector has not yet figured out how to do them consistently well. Governments will have to demonstrate leadership in network knowledge sharing; it is just too critical to network governance for public officials to wait around for the private sector to work out all the kinks.

Downsize and Upsize Simultaneously

Development of these core competencies, along with the aforementioned changes in business processes driven by technology, will have profound and far-reaching effects on the makeup of the public workforce. They boil down to this: government will need fewer people overall—particularly at the lower and middle levels—but more highly skilled individuals at the top.

The number of civil service jobs at the lower and middle levels of government will likely drop over time, and responsibilities will change. Many less-skilled tasks will be automated; others will be outsourced to the private sector, which will take over much of the routine and repetitive work. Many middle-management jobs either will become unnecessary as teams replace hierarchies or will be shifted to network partners that assume the role of coordinating people and information. Despite these major changes, the transition to government by network is not likely to involve substantial layoffs. Most governments will restructure their workforces through attrition—a luxury made possible by the retirement of the baby boomers and the resultant exodus of government employees. The bottom line: while many positions might be eliminated, few people will be fired and, on the whole, governments will still face huge skill-set shortages.

Solving these skill-set problems requires officials to consider major changes in how they deploy their workforces. Many governments today manufacture public services in a fashion that even manufacturers no longer believe appropriate—through narrow, repetitive tasks, accompanied by lots of supervision and little initiative. As governments shift over to managing providers, a challenging and important responsibility filled with opportunities where civil servants can make a difference, many public employees will be able to contribute more to public value, and will find more satisfaction in their jobs, but only if fundamental changes in human resource policies accompany this transformation.

First, skills should take precedence over job description. Second, to a much greater degree than possible today, employees need the ability to move from project to project without sacrificing career advancement. Highly restrictive human resource and civil service rules need to be changed to allow employees to bring broad skills to their assigned projects, unrestricted by the narrow "bands" in which they are employed.

A major part of the public sector workforce restructuring should involve attracting more people with sophisticated skills in team building, project management, risk analysis, negotiation, and other areas so critical to network governance. Today most governments do not have nearly enough individuals who can manage multiple partners with dexterity and adroitness, or who have sufficiently deep and broad relationships in the marketplace to know who should participate in providing the answer.

As we argued in chapter seven, the first thing government agencies will need to do to plug this gap is change government policies to encourage, not discourage, people from moving in and out of the public sector. This means restructuring retirement systems to allow more pension portability, and reinventing personnel systems to eliminate the strong bias against short-timers. Many states and the federal government have laws that appropriately prohibit employees from leaving and turning insider knowledge or relations into profit. But these laws often sweep so broadly and are enforced so bluntly that they inhibit talented individuals from doing stints in government. The public workforce needs more change and mobility: the ability to move within government less restrained by narrow work bands and differing tenure rules, as well as the ability to move from the outside into government to accomplish a project, without being penalized when leaving.

Second, the public sector will need to raise pay at the senior levels to attract more of the best and brightest. The skill sets government increasingly needs do not come cheap and, in some cases, can most likely be found in the top business and law schools. To attract this kind of talent, governments will have to compete with consulting firms, Fortune 500 companies, and investment banks for talent. This does not mean the public sector will have to achieve pay equity with these professions, but it will need to become more competitive. In the long run it will be much cheaper to pay more money to get the best people than to endure the continued project failures and billions of dollars' worth of wasted tax dollars that go along with poorly structured public-private partnerships.[5]

Conclusion

A complicated world, where individuals face highly complex, individualized problems, necessitates a new approach to delivering public services but also provides the necessary tools for the solution. Networked approaches produce both abundant opportunities for substantial improvements in public services and serious management challenges. We found many talented and innovative leaders who put together networks that produce enormous value. These capable public servants, the new face of the public sector, provide important lessons others would be wise to follow as, increasingly, democratic governance will mean relying on networks to enhance the quality of life for citizens around the world.

Acknowledgments

A serious book written in a compressed time frame nearly always is a team effort; *Governing by Network* is no exception. Many individuals worked diligently to make this book a reality, especially Jeannie Rhee and Marco Rodriguez, who both contributed hundreds of hours of research assistance at different stages of the book project. Without their enthusiasm, thoroughness, and hard work this book would not have been possible.

A number of Harvard colleagues provided key insights and support. Jack Donahue and Mark Moore, two of this country's most thoughtful and knowledgeable experts on public management, provided extensive and forthright comments when we needed them most. The book is better for their time and effort. Also from Harvard, Howard Husock pointed us to some excellent case studies, and graduate student Andy Feldman conducted important case study research. Last but not least, Melissa McKnight and Colette Labrador provided invaluable help coordinating and editing the dozens of case studies and interviews, and with other details.

Many of the cases featured in the book came to our attention through the Innovation in American Government Awards Program of Harvard University's Kennedy School of Government. This program, operated by the Roy and Lila Ash Institute for Democratic Governance and Innovation, fosters excellence in government around the world in order to generate and strengthen democracy. Through its Innovations Awards, the institute champions creative and effective governance and democratic practice. More information about the institute and its activities is available on its website, www.ashinstitute.harvard.edu.

Many Deloitte colleagues also played a vital role in making this book a reality. Hans Bossert read the manuscript and helped strengthen key sections of the book. Greg Pellegrino, Bob Campbell, and Ann Baxter provided crucial early backing; Ajit Kambil, much needed support in the latter stages. Dwight Allen, Michael Raynor, Robin Athey, and Joanne Gallagher reviewed parts of the manuscript and provided helpful comments. Frank Wilson, Mike Kerr, Paul Stephen, Bernard Nauta, David Rees, and Matt Even connected us to relevant case studies and provided important hands-on insights based on their experiences of working with government agencies.

Other friends and colleagues also played a role in making this book a reality. Geoff Segal from the Reason Foundation reviewed the entire manuscript and offered numerous beneficial suggestions. Particular thanks go to Skip Stitt, now with ACS, whose perspectives as a leading government reformer, and now commercial provider, proved exceptionally helpful.

We owe a special thanks to Don Kettl both for writing the foreword despite his grueling schedule and for his early words of encouragement when we were considering whether to write this book. Don's earlier books, such as *Sharing Power* and *Government by Proxy,* laid much of the intellectual groundwork on this subject.

We also want to thank the hundreds of public officials, corporate executives, community builders, nonprofit directors, scholars, and policy experts whom we interviewed in the course of writing *Governing by Network.* Much of what we have written we have learned from them. In particular, we would like to thank Lynn Scarlett, Brian O'Neill, Terri Shaw, Liam Sarsfield, Deidre Lee, Stan Soloway, and Jennifer Alexander.

At the Brookings Institution, Chris Kelaher shepherded the project from the concept stage to the end product and never wavered in his enthusiasm. Paul Light provided crucial support at critical times throughout. Managing editor Janet Walker moved the book from manuscript into production quickly—but always with the utmost care. Martha Gottron and

Teri Moore both, at different stages, did a superb editing job; Carlotta Ribar proofread the pages; and Julia Petrakis prepared the index.

As with any such work, the final product and all its shortcomings are wholly our own. The contribution of those listed above is not intended to imply accord with its conclusions.

Being the spouse of someone who is writing a book while holding down a full-time job is no easy task. For their endless patience and support, we would also like to thank our wives, Margaret and Jennifer, for enduring countless nights and weekends with our faces buried in our laptops when we should have been giving them our undivided attention. We hope the final product at least partly makes up for our absence. Steve would also like to thank his children, Olivia, Elizabeth, Reid, and Devereaux, who both inspired and tolerated three books and many political campaigns.

Notes

Several hundred interviews were conducted over the course of eighteen months for this book. Quotations for which no note is provided were taken from these interviews.

Foreword

1. "Concerns Raised That Changes in NASA Won't Last," *CNN.com*, August 26, 2003 (www.cnn.com/2003/TECH/space/08/26/sprj.colu.shuttle.report/).

Chapter 1

1. This premise is based on the belief, held by O'Neill and his management team, that a strong park is one that is an integral part of the surrounding community and one in which the community assumes some degree of ownership over improving and preserving the park.

2. George H. Frederickson, "The Repositioning of Public Administration," 1999 John Gaus Lecture, American Political Science Association (Atlanta, December 1999); and Laurence E. Lynn Jr., Carolyn Heinrich, and Carolyn J. Hill, *Governance and Performance: New Perspectives* (Georgetown University Press, 2000).

3. Lester Salamon, "The New Governance and the Tools of Public Action: An Introduction," in *The Tools of Government: A Guide to the New Governance,* edited by Lester Salamon (Oxford University Press, 2002), p. 3.

4. John Arquilla and David Ronfeldt, "Fighting the Network War," *Wired* (December 2001), p. 151.

5. In addition to these centers, there is also InfraGard, an association comprising the FBI, private companies, academic institutions, and state and local law enforcement agencies that share information about cyber security and critical infrastructure protection, and the National Cyber Security Partnership, which is composed of various business industry groups and government and academic experts.

6. S. E. Finer, *The History of Government: Ancient Monarchies and Empires*, vol. 1 (Oxford University Press, 1999), p. 351.

7. Lester Salamon provides a comprehensive survey of tools that can be used to facilitate third-party service delivery, including many that are exclusively financial, in Salamon, ed., *The Tools of Government: A Guide to the New Governance* (Oxford University Press, 2002).

8. Donald Kettl, *Sharing Power: Public Governance and Private Markets* (Brookings, 1993), p. 4.

9. William T. Woods, "Contract Management: Improving Services Acquisitions," GAO-02-179T (General Accounting Office, November 1, 2001), p. 1.

10. Paul Light, "Fact Sheet on the True Size of Government" (Brookings, September 2003), p. 4.

11. Office of Management and Budget, "Analytical Perspectives" and "Object Class Analysis," in *Budget of the United States Government, Fiscal Year 2005* (Government Printing Office, 2004).

12. Geoffrey F. Segal, Adrian T. Moore, and Adam B. Summers, "Competition and Government Services: Can Massachusetts Still Afford the Pacheco Law?" Pioneer Research Papers (Boston: Pioneer Institute, October 2002), p. iv.

13. John R. Bartle and Ronnie LaCourse Korosec, "Procurement and Contracting in State Government, 2000" (Syracuse University Government Performance Project, July 2001), p. 4.

14. J. Michael Quinlan, Charles W. Thomas, and Sherril Gautreaux, "The Privatization of Correctional Facilities," in *Privatizing Governmental Functions*, edited by Deborah Ballati (New York: Law Journal Press, 2001).

15. Nelson D. Schwartz, "The Pentagon's Private Army," *Fortune*, March 17, 2003.

16. Ian Mather, "War Inc. on the March to Relieve US Troops," *Scotland on Sunday*, July 20, 2003. The article cites these figures from Peter W. Singer's book *Corporate Warriors: The Rise of the Privatized Military Industry* (Cornell University Press, 2003).

17. Schwartz, "The Pentagon's Private Army." The article cites these figures from Singer's book *Corporate Warriors*.

18. Ibid.

19. Peter W. Singer, "Peacekeepers, Inc.," *Policy Review* 119 (June 2003): pp. 2–4.

20. Ariana Eunjung Cha and Ranae Merle, "Line Increasingly Blurred between Soldiers and Civilian Contractors," *Washington Post*, May 13, 2004, p. A16.

21. Singer, *Corporate Warriors*.

22. Cha and Merle, "Line Increasingly Blurred between Soldiers and Civilian Contractors."

23. Geoff Segal and others, "Privatization 2002, Annual Privatization Report" (Los Angles: Reason Public Policy Institute, 2003), pp. 30–31.

24. USAID (U.S. Agency for International Development), "Congo Basin Forest Partnership" (www.usaid.gov/about/wssd/congo.html [August 2002]).

25. Ibid.

26. M. Bryna Sanger, *The Welfare Marketplace: Privatization and Welfare Reform* (Brookings, 2003), p. 27.

27. Commission on Public Private Partnerships, *Building Better Partnerships: The Final Report of the Commission on Public-Private Partnerships* (London: Institute for Public Policy Research, 2001), p. 70.

28. U.K. Cabinet Office, "Wiring It Up: Whitehall's Management of Cross-cutting Policies and Services" (London: U.K. Performance and Innovation Unit, December 2000), p. 3.

29. Social Exclusion Unit, "What Is SEU?" (www.socialexclusionunit.gov.uk/what_is_SEU.htm [January 2004]).

30. Social Exclusion Unit, "Review of the Social Exclusion Unit" (www.socialexclusionunit.gov.uk/publications/reports/html/review.htm [January 2004]).

31. Ronald H. Coase, "The Nature of the Firm," *Economica* 4 (November, 1937), pp. 386–405.

32. Bob Tedeschi, "Coase's Ideas Flourish in the New Economy," *New York Times*, October 2, 2000.

33. Ronald H. Coase, "The Problem of Social Cost," *Journal of Law and Economics* 3 (1960), pp. 1–44.

34. Tedeschi, "Coase's Ideas Flourish in the New Economy."

35. David S. Alberts, John J. Garstka, and Frederick P. Stein, *Network Centric Warfare: Developing and Leveraging Information Superiority,* 2nd ed. (Department of Defense Cooperative Research Program, 2000).

36. Ryan Streeter, "The Neighborhood Empowerment Initiative in Three Indianapolis Neighborhoods: Practices as Principles," in *Putting Faith in Neighborhoods: Making Cities Work through Grassroots Citizenship*, edited by Stephen Goldsmith (Noblesville, Ind.: Hudson Institute, 2002), pp. 147–87.

37. Donald F. Kettl, "Managing Indirect Government," in *The Tools of Government: A Guide to the New Governance,* edited by Lester Salamon (Oxford University Press, 2002), p. 492.

38. Keith Provan and H. Brinton Milward, "Do Networks Really Work? A Framework for Evaluating Public-Sector Organizational Networks," *Public Administration Review* 61(July, 2001), pp. 414–23; H. Brinton Milward, Introduction to "Symposium on the Hollow State: Capacity, Control, and Performance in Interorganizational Settings," *Journal of Public Administration Research and Theory* 6 (April, 1996), pp. 193–95; and H. Brinton Milward and Keith G. Provan, "How Networks Are Governed," in *Governance and Performance: New Perspectives*, edited by Laurence E. Lynn Jr., Carolyn Heinrich, and Carolyn J. Hill (Georgetown University Press, 2000), pp. 330–36.

39. Kettl, *Sharing Power*, pp. 22–40.

40. We have included many of the best writings on governing by network in the bibliography. Despite the growing academic literature on government and networks, we believe there still is a comparative shortage of practical texts that public managers can use to help them actually manage a government of networks.

41. Other influential books that explore the right organization for public action include John D. Donahue, *The Privatization Decision: Public Ends, Private Mean* (New York: Basic Books, 1989); George H. Frederickson, *The Spirit of Public Administration* (San Francisco: Jossey-Bass, 1996); Donald F. Kettl, *Sharing Power: Public Governance and Private Markets* (Brookings, 1993); Vincent Ostrom, *The Intellectual Crisis of Public Administration* (University of Alabama Press, 1973); Lester Salamon, ed., *The Tools of Government: A Guide to the New Governance* (Oxford University Press, 2002); and Herbert A. Simon, *Administrative Behavior*, 3rd ed. (New York: Free Press, 1976). Among the more prolific academics in this field are Perri 6 (Kings College, United Kingdom), Robert Agranoff (Indiana University), John D. Donahue (Harvard University), Donald F. Kettl (University of Pennsylvania), Walter J. M. Kickert (Erasmus University, Netherlands), Michael McGuire (University of North Texas), H. Brinton Milward (University of Arizona), Keith Provan (University of Arizona), Lester Salamon (Johns Hopkins University), and E. S. Savas (Baruch College).

42. See, for example, William D. Eggers and John O'Leary, *Revolution at the Roots: Making Our Government Smaller, Better and Closer to Home* (New York: Free Press, 1995); and Stephen Goldsmith, *The Twenty-First Century City: Resurrecting Urban America* (Washington: Regnery, 1997).

43. Russell M. Linden, *Working across Boundaries: Making Collaboration Work in Government and Nonprofit Organizations* (San Francisco: Jossey-Bass, 2002), pp. 11–12.

Chapter 2

1. R. Kent Weaver, *Ending Welfare as We Know It* (Brookings, 2000), p. 343; and Rebecca J. Swartz and Thomas Corbett, "W-2 Achievements and Challenges: An Overview and Interpretation of the White Papers Commissioned by the Department of Workforce Development," University of Wisconsin–Madison, Institute for Research on Policy, 2001, p. 2.

2. David Dodenhoff, "Privatizing Welfare in Wisconsin: Ending Administrative Entitlements—W-2's Untold Story," Wisconsin Policy Research Institute Report 11 (Milwaukee: January 1998), p.14.

3. Jeffrey H. Dyer, *Collaborative Advantage: Winning through Extended Enterprise Supplier Networks* (Oxford University Press, 2000), p. 5.

4. For an extensive discussion of Toyota's supply chain relationship model, see Dyer, *Collaborative Advantage.*

5. Stephen Goldsmith, *The Twenty-First Century City: Resurrecting Urban America* (Washington: Regnery, 1997), pp. 30–44.

6. For an excellent discussion of the challenges to innovating within government, see James Q. Wilson, *Bureaucracy* (New York: Basic Books, 1989), pp. 218–32. For an analysis of the challenges to innovation within large organizations in general, see Clayton M. Christensen and Michael E. Raynor, *The Innovator's Solution: Creating and Sustaining Successful Growth* (Harvard Business School Press, 2003), pp. 9–11. For an excellent discussion of internal networks, see Rosabeth Moss Kanter, *The Change Masters* (New York: Simon and Schuster, 1982).

7. Elaine C. Kamarck, "Applying 21st-Century Government to the Challenge of Homeland Security" (Washington: IBM Endowment for the Business of Government, June 2002), p. 12.

8. See, for example, Leslie M. Groves, *Now It Can Be Told: The Story of the Manhattan Project* (New York: Da Capo Press, 1962), chapters 4–7.

9. Dyer, *Collaborative Advantage*, pp. 59–83.

10. Russell M. Linden, *Working across Boundaries: Making Collaboration Work in Government and Nonprofit Organizations* (San Francisco: Jossey-Bass, 2002), p. 13.

11. H. Brinton Milward, Introduction to "Symposium on the Hollow State: Capacity, Control, and Performance in Interorganizational Settings," *Journal of Public Administration Research and Theory* 6 (April 1996), p. 194.

12. Department of Energy, "The Atomic Energy Commission and Postwar Biomedical Radiation Research" (tis.eh.doe.gov/ohre/roadmap/achre/intro_4.html [March 2004]).

13. Paul Light, *The True Size of Government* (Brookings, 1999), p. 102.

14. Ibid.

15. Ibid., p. 103.

16. Shawn Zeller, "Smashing the System," *Government Executive* (November 2003), p. 34.

17. Linden, *Working across Boundaries*, pp. 14–15.

18. Robert Agranoff and Michael McGuire, "Multi-Network Management: Collaboration and the Hollow State in Local Economic Policy," *Journal of Public Administration Research and Theory* 8 (January 1998), pp. 67–91.

19. Internal Revenue Service, "Number of Individual Income Tax Returns Filed Electronically and Accepted, by State, Fiscal Year 2002," *2002 IRS Data Book* (March 2003).

20. Stephen Goldsmith, *Putting Faith in Neighborhoods: Making Cities Work through Grassroots Citizenship* (Noblesville, Ind.: Hudson Institute, 2002); and Lester M. Salamon, *Partners in Public Service: Government-Nonprofit Cooperation in the Modern Welfare State* (Johns Hopkins University Press, 1995).

Chapter 3

1. H. Brinton Milward and Keith G. Provan, "How Networks Are Governed," in *Governance and Performance: New Perspectives*, edited by Laurence E. Lynn, Jr., Carolyn Heinrich, and Carolyn J. Hill (Georgetown University Press, 2000), pp. 316–17.

2. Mark Moore, e-mail to authors, May 9, 2004.

3. Eugene Bardach, *Getting Agencies to Work Together: The Practice and Theory of Managerial Craftsmanship* (Brookings, 1998), pp. 131–34.

4. Gregg Keizer, "Outsourcing: A 50-50 Proposition," *Information Week*, March 26, 2003 (www.informationweek.com/story/IWK20030326S0006).

5. Paul Kaihla, "Inside Cisco's $2 Billion Blunder," *Business 2.0*, March 2002 (www.business2.com/b2/web/articles/0,17863,514495,00.html).

6. Marianne Kolbasuk McGee, "The Bioterrorism Threat Is Forcing Health Care to Lose Its Aversion to IT," *Information Week*, November 19, 2001, p. 52.

7. Phillip J. Cooper, "Moving beyond Advocacy in Public-Private Partnerships," in *The Leadership Challenge: Effective Organizations in the 21st Century*, edited by Patrick Boyer (Guelph, Ontario: Guelph University, 2002), pp. 127–44.

8. Milward and Provan, "How Networks Are Governed," p. 329.

9. H. Brinton Milward, Keith G. Provan, and Barbara A. Else, "What Does the 'Hollow State' Look Like?" in *Public Management: The State of the Art*, edited by Barry Bozeman (San Francisco: Jossey-Bass, 1993); H. Brinton Milward, Introduction to "Symposium on the Hollow State: Capacity, Control, and Performance in Interorganizational Settings," *Journal of Public Administration Research and Theory* 6 (1996), pp. 193–95; and H. Brinton Milward, "Nonprofit Contracting and the Hollow State," *Public Administration Review* 54 (1994), pp. 1–73.

10. Donald F. Kettl, "Managing Indirect Government," in *The Tools of Government: A Guide to the New Governance*, edited by Lester Salamon (Oxford University Press, 2002), p. 499.

11. Karen Robb, "Too Many Projects, Too Few Chiefs," *Federal Times*, December 1, 2003, p. 1.

12. David Phinney, "Senate Committee Welcomes Procurement Nominee," *Federal Times*, May 3, 2004; and U.S. General Accounting Office, "Acquisition Workforce: Status of Agency Efforts to Address Future Needs," Report to Senate Committee on Governmental Affairs, GAO-03-55, December 2002.

Chapter 4

1. Robert Agranoff and Michael McGuire, "Big Questions in Network Management Research," paper prepared for the Fifth National Public Management Research Conference, Texas A&M University, December 3–4, 1999, pp. 2–3. In public-private networks, either government or a third party designs the network,

while the role of activator is usually performed by a senior government official or politician.

2. Phillip J. Cooper, *Governing by Contract: Challenges and Opportunities for Public Managers* (Washington: CQ Press, 2003), p. 117.

3. For a different typology of networks, see Robert Agranoff, "Leveraging Networks: A Guide for Public Managers Working across Organizations" (Washington: IBM Endowment for the Business of Government, 2003).

4. The MVD is responsible for vehicle registration, titles, registration renewal, vehicle inspections, driver license issuance, and a variety of transportation-related permits.

5. Keith Provan and Brinton Milward, "Do Networks Really Work? A Framework for Evaluating Public-Sector Organizational Networks," *Public Administration Review* 61 (2001), pp. 414–23.

6. Steven J. Kelman, "Deregulating Federal Procurement: Nothing to Fear but Discretion Itself?" In *Deregulating the Public Service*, edited by John J. DiIulio Jr. (Brookings, 1994), pp. 102–28.

7. G. Thomas Kingsley and others, "Lessons from HOPE VI for the Future of Public Housing: A Working Paper" (Washington: Urban Institute, August 2003).

8. Richard W. Walker, "CIOs Take a New Approach, Put Performance First," *Government Computer News*, January 27, 2003. www.gcn.com/22_2/mgmt_edition/20910-1.html.

9. Ibid.

10. H. Brinton Milward, Introduction to "Symposium on the Hollow State: Capacity, Control, and Performance in Interorganizational Settings," *Journal of Public Administration Research and Theory* 6 (April 1996), p. 193; and H. Brinton Milward and Keith G. Provan, "Private Principals, Nonprofit Agents," paper prepared for the American Political Science Association annual meeting, Boston, Mass., August-September 2002.

11. Deloitte Research, "Relationship Portfolio for the Public Sector: A Strategic Approach to Partnering in Turbulent Times" (New York: 2002), p. 17.

12. Paul Hirst, "Democracy and Governance," in *Debating Governance*, edited by Jon Pierre (Oxford University Press, 2000), chapter 3.

Chapter 5

1. Kirsten Lundberg, "Charting a Course in a Storm: The US Postal Service and the Anthrax Crisis," Kennedy School of Government Case Program C-15-03-1692.0, 2003. 28 (Harvard University, 2003).

2. Because many of TSA's 400 internal and external constituents may have a need to share "sensitive" information, the information sharing system is set up for role-based access. See Deloitte, "TSA: We Will Never Assume We've Got the Job Done," New York, 2002, p. 23.

3. Deloitte Research and Stanford Global Supply Chain Management Forum, *Integrating Demand and Supply Chains in the Global Automotive Industry: Creating a Digital Loyalty Network at General Motors Deloitte* (New York: Deloitte Research, and Stanford University, 2003), p. 16.

4. M. Mitchell Waldrop, "Can Sense-Making Keep Us Safe?" *Technology Review*, March 2003, p. 45.

5. Center for Digital Government, "PA-NEDSS: A Case Study"(Folsom, Calif.: 2004).

6. Ibid., p. 3.

7. William C. Ouchi, *The M-Form Society: How American Teamwork Can Capture the Competitive Edge* (Reading, Mass.: Addison-Wesley, 1984); and Fritz W. Scharpf, 1993, "Coordination in Hierarchies and Networks," in *Games in Hierarchies and Networks: Analytical and Empirical Approaches to the Study of Governance Institutions*, edited by Fritz W. Scharpf (Boulder, Colo.: Westview Press, 1993).

8. Joan Magretta, "The Power of Virtual Integration: Interview with Michael Dell," *Harvard Business Review*, vol. 76 (March–April 1998), pp. 72–84.

9. Jeffrey H. Dyer, *Collaborative Advantage: Winning through Extended Enterprise Supplier Networks* (Oxford University Press, 2000), pp. 59–83.

10. C. O'Dell, and C. Jackson Grayson Jr., *If Only We Knew What We Know: The Transfer of Internal Knowledge and Best Practice* (New York: Free Press, 1998).

11. Andrew Campbell, "The Federal Aviation Administration's Knowledge Services Network: A SharePoint Case Study," Applied Knowledge Group, Inc., 2003 (www.microsoft.com/resources/casestudies/CaseStudy.asp?casestudyid=156).

12. William M. Snyder and Etienne Wenger, "Our World as a Learning System: A Communities-of-Practice Approach," in *Creating a Learning Culture: Strategy, Technology, and Practice*, edited by Marcia L. Conner and James G. Clawson (Cambridge University Press, 2004).

13. Jordan D. Lewis, *Trusted Partners: How Companies Build Mutual Trust and Win Together* (New York: Free Press, 1999), pp. 161–72.

14. Jordan D. Lewis, *The Connected Corporation: How Leading Companies Win through Customer-Supplier Alliances* (New York: Free Press, 1995), pp. 30–8.

15. Michael Hardy, "Managing the Contractors," *Federal Computer Week*, November 10, 2003 (www.fcw.com/fcw/articles/2003/1110/tec-manage-11-10-03.asp).

16. Ibid.

17. ACS, as the prime contractor, needed to merge the separate "legacy" systems into an integrated data store. The subject matter expertise of each component of the solution resided in the legacy teams of the firms that had previously delivered work for the division (for example, EDS Loan Consolidations, ACS Loan Processing). One of the authors, Stephen Goldsmith, provides strategic advice to ACS.

Chapter 6

1. Liverpool Partnership Group, *LSP Accreditation – LPG's Self Assessment* (January 2002).

2. Jeffrey H. Dyer, *Collaborative Advantage: Winning through Extended Enterprise Supplier Networks* (Oxford University Press, 2000).

3. Ibid., p. 38. Dyer shows empirically the correlation between higher supplier trust and lower transaction costs in a study of U.S. and Japanese automakers. Transaction costs are defined as the costs associated with staff time spent on activities such as negotiating and assigning blame.

4. Donna Harrington-Lueker, "The High Flyer Falls," *American School Board Journal*, April 1996, p. 32.

5. Jordan D. Lewis, *Trusted Partners: How Companies Build Mutual Trust and Win Together* (New York: Free Press, 1999).

6. See the extensive literature on transactional cost economics and principal-agent theory, including Oliver E. Williamson, *Markets and Hierarchies* (New York: Free Press, 1975); and Arman Alchian and Harold Demsetz, "Production, Information Costs, and Economic Organization," *American Economic Review* 62 (1972), pp. 777–95. Also see E. S. Savas, *Privatization: The Key to Better Government* (Chatham, N.J.: Chatham House Publishers, 1987), and Robert D. Behn and Peter A. Kant, "Strategies for Avoiding the Pitfalls of Performance Contracting," *Public Productivity and Management Review,* 22 (June 1999), pp. 470–89.

7. Reynolds Holding, "Medicare Bilked for Billions in Bogus Claims," *San Francisco Chronicle,* January 12, 2003, p. A1.

8. Ibid.

9. Stephen Goldsmith, *The Twenty-First Century City: Resurrecting Urban America* (Washington: Regnery, 1997), pp. 58–63.

10. Anitha Reddy, "Sharing Savings, and Risk," *Washington Post*, February 16, 2004, p. E1.

11. "Wisconsin Welfare to Work Agencies Lacking Funds," Associated Press, April 27, 2004.

12. John D. Donahue, *The Privatization Decision: Public Ends, Private Means* (New York: Basic Books, 1989), pp. 198–201.

13. Behn and Kant, "Strategies for Avoiding the Pitfalls of Performance Contracting."

14. General Accounting Office, "Contract Management: Commercial Use of Share-in-Savings Contracting," GAO-03-327 (January 31, 2003).

15. Bill Reinhardt, "Koch Signs 20-Year State Highway Warranty," *Public Works Financing* (July/August 1998), p. 1.

16. David B. Rosenbaum, "Fast Quake Recovery Redeemed State Transportation Department," *Engineering News Record* (January 16, 1995), p. 33.

17. William D. Eggers, "Performance-Based Contracting," How-To Guide 17 (Los Angeles: Reason Public Policy Institute, 1997), p. 22.

18. H. Brinton Milward and Keith G. Provan, "How Networks Are Governed," in *Governance and Performance: New Perspectives*, edited by Laurence E. Lynn Jr., Carolyn Heinrich, and Carolyn J. Hill (Georgetown University Press, 2000).

19. Behn and Kant, "Strategies for Avoiding the Pitfalls of Performance Contracting."

20. See, for example, Karen Robb and David Phinney, "Contracting Shortcuts, Violations Rampant at GSA," *Federal Times*, April 26, 2004, p. 8; and David Phinney, "The Dark Side of Acquisition Reform: Diminished Oversight Leads to Overpricing," *Federal Times*, April 5, 2004, p. 1.

21. Electronic Data Systems did the loan originations, Affiliated Computer Systems did the payment processing, Raytheon handled the collections component, and DCS Pearson operated several of the call centers.

22. Deloitte and Touche, 2002 Economic Intelligence Unit Survey of FTSE (London Stock Exchange) 500 Companies, London, 2002.

23. Deloitte and Touche, "Extending the Enterprise: Managing Alliances Successfully," New York, July 2003.

Chapter 7

1. Robert Agranoff and Michael McGuire, "After the Network Is Formed: Process, Power, and Performance," in *Getting Results through Collaboration*, edited by Myrna Mandell (Westport, Conn.: Quorum Books, 2001), p. 13.

2. At the federal level in the United States, the acquisition workforce has fallen by 22 percent over the past decades. See U.S. General Accounting Office, "Acquisition Workforce: Status of Agency Efforts to Address Future Needs," Report to Senate Committee on Governmental Affairs, GAO-03-55 (December 2002), p. 1.

3. David Osborne and Ted Gaebler, *Reinventing Government* (Reading, Mass.: Addison-Wesley, 1992), introductory chapter.

4. Strategic Partnering Task Force, "Rethinking Service Delivery: Volume Five" (London: Office of the Deputy Prime Minister, December 21, 2003), p. 18.

5. Paul Light, *The New Public Service* (Brookings, 1999), p. 8.

6. Donald E. Kettl, *The Global Public Management Revolution: A Report on the Transformation of Governance* (Brookings, 2000), p 22.

7. Brent Schlender, "Peter Drucker Sets Us Straight," *Fortune*, December 29, 2003.

8. Light, *The New Public Service*, pp. 19–102.

9. One of the authors worked with Lynn Scarlett at the Reason Foundation.

10. Donald F. Kettl, "Managing Indirect Government," in *The Tools of Government: A Guide to the New Governance*, edited by Lester Salamon (Oxford University Press, 2002), p. 499.

11. U.S. General Accounting Office, "Acquisition Workforce," p. 14.

12. Cleaning up these small signs of social decay was the first step taken by many mayors, including New York mayor Rudolph Giuliani in efforts to reduce crime; the effort typically involved various city agencies working together.

13. See, for example: Kettl, "Managing Indirect Government," p. 507.

14. Phillip J. Cooper, *Governing by Contract: Challenges and Opportunities for Public Managers* (Washington: CQ Press, 2003), p. 169.

15. Ibid., p. 168.

Chapter 8

1. Jessica Lipnack and Jeffrey Stamps, *The Age of the Network: Organizing Principles for the 21st Century* (Essex Junction, Vt.: Oliver Wright Publications, 1994).

2. Generally, government does not measure internal performance rigorously enough, nor do its senior managers always have the tools to enforce accountability.

3. Michael Hammer, "Deep Change: How Operational Innovation Can Transform Your Company," *Harvard Business Review*, vol. 82 (April 2004), pp. 84–93.

4. C. K. Prahalad and Venkat Ramaswamy, *The Future of Competition: Co-Creating Unique Value with Customers* (Harvard Business School Press, 2004).

5. Only a few governments have been courageous enough to wade into the politically treacherous waters of changing pay systems. The most successful have been governments in Australia and New Zealand, both of which set about attracting top corporate executives into government through higher pay in the midst of major downsizing programs. The essence of the deal these governments offered to the legislature and the public at large was that many individual salaries would go up but the overall wage bill for public employees would go down. The New Zealand government, for example, reduced the number of employees by 35 percent during the 1980s and 1990s at the same time it sharply raised the pay for certain positions. Moreover, typically at least 10–15 percent of each executive's salary was made at risk, depending on performance; bonuses of up to 20 percent could be earned for superior performance. While political leaders in both countries knew that they would take a political hit from raising the salaries of senior management and certain specialists, they felt they had no choice but to do so. Both governments had embarked on far-reaching public sector reform programs, and they simply did not have the skills in-house to effectively carry out such an ambitious program. Moreover, policymakers reasoned that the public in time would accept reform so long as government services and operations improved. The goal was neither to reward mediocrity nor to create windfalls, but to raise the level of talent in government and create a more performance-based compensation system.

Selected Bibliography

6, Perri, *Holistic Government* (London: Demos, 1997).

Agranoff, Robert, "Leveraging Networks: A Guide for Public Managers Working across Organizations" (Washington: IBM Endowment for the Business of Government, 2003).

Agranoff, Robert, and Michael McGuire, "Multi-Network Management: Collaboration and the Hollow State in Local Economic Policy," *Journal of Public Administration Research and Theory* 8 (1998): 67–91.

———, "Big Questions in Network Management Research," paper prepared for the Fifth National Public Management Research Conference (Texas A&M University, December 3–4, 1999).

———, "After the Network Is Formed: Process, Power, and Performance," in *Getting Results through Collaboration,* edited by Myrna Mandell (Westport, Conn.: Quorum Books, 2001).

———, *Collaborative Public Management: New Strategies for Local Governments* (Georgetown University Press, 2003).

Alberts, David S., John J. Garstka, and Frederick P. Stein, *Network Centric Warfare: Developing and Leveraging Information Superiority,* 2nd ed. (Department of Defense Cooperative Research Program, 2000).

Alchian, Arman, and Harold Demsetz, "Production, Information Costs, and Economic Organization," *American Economic Review* 62 (1972): 777–95.

Austen, James, *The Collaboration Challenge: How Nonprofits and Businesses Succeed through Strategic Alliances* (San Francisco: Jossey-Bass, 2000).

Barabasi, Albert-Laszlo, *Linked: The New Science of Networks* (Cambridge, Mass.: Perseus Publishing, 2002).

Bardach, Eugene, *Getting Agencies to Work Together: The Practice and Theory of Managerial Craftsmanship* (Brookings, 1998).

Bardach, Eugene, and Cara Lesser, "Accountability in Human Service Collaboratives—And to Whom?" *Journal of Public Administration Research and Theory* 6 (1996): 197–224.

Barzelay, Michael, *Breaking through Bureaucracy* (University of California Press, 1992).

Behn, Robert D., and Peter A. Kant, "Strategies for Avoiding the Pitfalls of Performance Contracting," *Public Productivity and Management Review* (June 1999): 470–89.

Berger, Peter, and Richard John Neuhaus, "Mediating Structures and the Dilemmas of the Welfare State," in *To Empower People: From State to Civil Society*, edited by Michael Novak (Washington: American Enterprise Institute, 1996): 257–64.

Boris, Elizabeth T., and C. Eugene Steuerle, *Nonprofits and Government: Collaboration and Conflict* (Washington: Urban Institute, 1999).

Boston, Jonathan, and others, *Public Management: The New Zealand Mode* (Oxford University Press, 1996).

Bozeman, Barry, ed., *Public Management: The State of the Art* (San Francisco: Jossey-Bass, 1993).

Coase, Ronald H., "The Nature of the Firm," *Economica* 4 (1937): 386–405.

———, "The Problem of Social Cost," *Journal of Law and Economics* 3 (1960): 1–44.

Commission on Public Private Partnerships, *Building Better Partnerships: The Final Report of the Commission on Public Private Partnerships* (London: Institute for Public Policy Research, 2001).

Cooper, Phillip J., *Governing by Contract: Challenges and Opportunities for Public Managers* (Washington: CQ Press, 2003).

Crawford, John W. Jr., and Steven L. Krahn, "The Demanding Customer and the Hollow Organization: Meeting Today's Contract Management Challenge," *Public Productivity and Management Review* 22 (September 1998): 107–18.

DiIulio, John J., Gerald Garvey, and Donald Kettl, *Improving Government Performance: An Owner's Manual* (Brookings, 1993).

DiIulio, John J., and others, "The Public Administration of James Q. Wilson: A Symposium on Bureaucracy," *Public Administration Review* 51, no. 3 (1991): 193–201.

Dionne, E. J., and Ming Hsu Chen. eds., *Sacred Places, Civic Purposes: Should Government Help Faith-Based Charity?* (Brookings, 2001).

Donahue, John D., *The Privatization Decision: Public Ends, Private Means* (New York: Basic Books, 1989).

Donahue, John D., and Joseph S. Nye Jr., *Market-Based Governance: Supply Side, Demand Side, Upside, and Downside* (Brookings, 2002).

Drucker, Peter, "The Deadly Sins in Public Administration," *Public Administration Review* (March/April 1980): 103–6.

Dyer, Jeffrey H., *Collaborative Advantage: Winning through Extended Enterprise Supplier Networks* (Oxford University Press, 2000).

Eggers, William D., and John O'Leary, *Revolution at the Roots: Making Our Government Smaller, Better and Closer to Home* (New York: Free Press, 1995).

Feldman, Martha S., and Anne M. Khadenian, "Principles for Public Management Practice: From Dichotomies to Interdependence," *Governance: An International Journal of Policy and Administration* 14, no. 3 (2001): 339–61.

Frederickson, George H., "The Repositioning of Public Administration," John Gaus Lecture (Atlanta: American Political Science Association, December 1999).

———, *The Spirit of Public Administration* (San Francisco: Jossey-Bass, 1996).

Frumkin, Peter, and Alice Andre-Clark, "When Missions, Markets, and Politics Collide: Value and Strategy in the Nonprofit Human Services," *Nonprofit and Voluntary Sector Quarterly* 29, no. 1 (2000): 141–63.

Garvey, Gerald, *Facing the Bureaucracy: Living and Dying in a Public Agency* (San Francisco: Jossey-Bass, 1993).

Gates, Scott, and Jeffrey Hill, "Democratic Accountability and Governmental Innovation in the Use of Nonprofit Organizations," *Policy Studies Review* 14, no. 1 (1995): 137–48.

Goldsmith, Stephen, *The Twenty-First Century City: Resurrecting Urban America* (Washington: Regnery, 1997).

———, *Putting Faith in Neighborhoods: Making Cities Work through Grassroots Citizenship* (Noblesville, Ind.: Hudson Institute, 2002).

Goodsell, Charles, *The Case for Bureaucracy: A Public Administration Polemic* (Chatham, N.J.: Chatham House Publishers, 1994).

Heinrich, Carolyn, and Carolyn J. Hill, "The Empirical Study of Governance: Theoretical Methods," paper presented at the Workshop on Models and Methods for the Empirical Study of Governance (University of Arizona, 1999).

Kamensy, John M., and Thomas J. Burlin, *Collaboration: Using Networks and Partnerships* (Lanham, Md.: Rowman and Littlefield, 2004).

Kelman, Steven J., "Deregulating Federal Procurement: Nothing to Fear but Discretion Itself?" in *Deregulating the Public Service,* edited by John J. DiIulio Jr. (Brookings, 1994).

Kettl, Donald F., *Sharing Power: Public Governance and Private Markets* (Brookings, 1993).

———, *Government by Proxy: (Mis?)Managing Federal Programs* (Washington: Congressional Quarterly Press, 1998).

———, *The Global Public Management Revolution: A Report on the Transformation of Governance* (Brookings, 2000).

———, "Managing Indirect Government," in *The Tools of Government: A Guide to the New Governance,* edited by Lester Salamon (Oxford University Press, 2002): 490–511.

————, *The Transformation of Governance: Public Administration for Twenty-First Century America* (Johns Hopkins University Press, 2002).

Kettl, Donald F., and others, *Civil Service Reform: Building a Government That Works* (Brookings, 1996).

Kickert, Walter J. M., Erik Hans Klijn, and Joop F. M. Koppenjan, *Managing Complex Networks: Strategies for the Public Sector* (Thousand Oaks, Calif.: Sage Publications, 1997).

Lewis, Jordan D., *The Connected Corporation: How Leading Companies Win through Customer-Supplier Alliances* (New York: Free Press, 1995).

————, *Trusted Partners: How Companies Build Mutual Trust and Win Together* (New York: Free Press, 1999).

Light, Paul, *The True Size of Government* (Brookings, 1998).

————, *The New Public Service* (Brookings, 1999).

Linden, Russell M., *Working across Boundaries: Making Collaboration Work in Government and Nonprofit Organizations* (San Francisco: Jossey-Bass, 2002).

Lipnack, Jessica, and Jeffrey Stamps, *The Age of the Network: Organizing Principles for the 21st Century* (Essex Junction, Vt.: Oliver Wright Publications, 1994).

Lynn, Laurence E., Jr., Carolyn Heinrich, and Carolyn J. Hill, *Governance and Performance: New Perspectives* (Georgetown University Press, 2000).

Mandell, Myrna, *Getting Results through Collaboration* (Westport, Conn.: Quorum Books, 2001).

McGuire, Michael, "Managing Networks: Propositions on What Managers Do and Why They Do It," *Public Administration Review* 62 (September/October 2002): 599–609.

Miles, Raymond E., and Charles C. Snow, "Causes of Failure in Network Organizations," *California Management Review* 34, no. 4 (1996): 53–72.

Milward, H. Brinton, Introduction to "Symposium on the Hollow State: Capacity, Control, and Performance in Interorganizational Settings," *Journal of Public Administration Research and Theory* 6 (1996): 193–95.

————, "Nonprofit Contracting and the Hollow State," *Public Administration Review* 54 (1994): 1–73.

Milward, H. Brinton, and Keith G. Provan, "Governing the Hollow State," *Journal of Public Administration Research and Theory* 10 (February 2000): 359–79.

————, "How Networks Are Governed," in *Governance and Performance: New Perspectives*, edited by Laurence E. Lynn Jr., Carolyn Heinrich, and Carolyn J. Hill (Georgetown University Press, 2000).

————, "Managing the Hollow State: Collaboration and Contracting," University of Arizona School of Public Administration and Policy, 2001.

————, "Private Principals, Nonprofit Agents," paper presented at American Political Science Association annual meeting (Boston, August-September, 2002).

Moe, Terry, "The New Economics of Organization," *American Journal of Political Science* 28, no. 4 (1984): 739–77.

Morgan, Gareth, *Images of Organization* (Beverly Hills, Calif.: Sage, 1986).

Niskanen, William, *Bureaucracy and Representative Government* (Chicago: Aldine, 1971).

Nohria, Nitin, and Sumantra Ghoshal, *The Differentiated Network: Organizing Multinational Corporations for Value Creation* (San Francisco: Jossey-Bass Publishers, 1997).

Ostrom, Vincent, *The Intellectual Crisis of Public Administration* (University of Alabama Press, 1973).

O'Toole, Laurence J., "Treating Networks Seriously: Practical and Research-Based Agendas in Public Administration," *Public Administration Review* 57 (1997): 45–52.

Ouchi, William C., *The M-Form Society: How American Teamwork Can Capture the Competitive Edge* (Reading, Mass.: Addison-Wesley, 1984).

Peters, Tom, *Liberation Management: Necessary Disorganization for the Nanosecond Nineties* (New York: Knopf, 1992).

————, *The Tom Peters Seminar: Crazy Times Call for Crazy Organizations* (New York: Vintage, 1994).

Powell, Walter W., "Neither Market nor Hierarchy: Network Forms of Organization," in *Organizational Behavior,* edited by B. Staw and L. Cummings (Greenwich, Conn.: JAI Press, 1990).

Provan, Keith, and H. Brinton Milward, "Do Networks Really Work? A Framework for Evaluating Public-Sector Organizational Networks," *Public Administration Review* 61 (2001): 414–23.

Rehfuss, John A., *Contracting Out in Government: A Guide to Working with Outside Contractors to Supply Public Services* (San Francisco: Jossey-Bass Publishers, 1989).

Rosenau, Pauline Vaillancourt, *Public-Private Policy Partnerships* (MIT Press, 2000).

Salamon, Lester, "The New Governance and the Tools of Public Action: An Introduction," in *The Tools of Government: A Guide to the New Governance,* edited by Lester Salamon (Oxford University Press, 2002).

————, *Partners in Public Service: Government-Nonprofit Cooperation in the Modern Welfare State* (Johns Hopkins University Press, 1995).

————, *The Resilient Sector: The State of Nonprofit America* (Brookings, 2003).

Sanger, M. Bryna, *The Welfare Marketplace: Privatization and Welfare Reform* (Brookings, 2003).

Savas, E. S., *Privatization: The Key to Better Government* (Chatham, N.J.: Chatham House Publishers, 1987).

Scharpf, Fritz W., "Coordination in Hierarchies and Networks," in *Games in Hierarchies and Networks: Analytical and Empirical Approaches to the Study of Governance Institutions,* edited by Fritz W. Scharpf (Boulder, Colo.: Westview, 1993).

Schwartz, Robert, "Managing Government: Third Sector Collaboration: Accountability, Ambiguity, and Politics," *International Journal of Public Administration* 24, no. 11 (2001): 1161–88.

Simon, Herbert A., *Administrative Behavior* (New York: Free Press, 1976).

Skowronek, Stephen, *Building a New American State: The Expansion of National Administrative Capacities, 1877–1920* (Cambridge University Press, 1982).

Smith, Stephen Rathgeb, and Michael Lipsky, *Nonprofits for Hire: The Welfare State in the Age of Contracting* (Harvard University Press, 1993).

Stoker, Gerry, Perri 6, Kimberley Stelzer, and Diana Leat, *Towards Holistic Governance* (Hampshire, England: Palgrave Macmillan, 2002).

Streeter, Ryan, "The Future of Government Partnerships with the Faith Community," in *Religion and the Public Square in the 21st Century: Proceedings from the Conference* (Washington: Hudson Institute, 2001).

Tullock, Gordon, *The Politics of Bureaucracy* (Washington: Public Affairs Press, 1965).

Williamson, Oliver E., *Markets and Hierarchies* (New York: Free Press, 1975).

Wilson, James Q., *Bureaucracy* (New York: Basic Books, 1989).

Index

Abu Ghraib prison. *See* Iraq
Accountability: adaptive management and, 150–51; audit and control mechanisms, 122–24; creaming, 134; fraud, 146; goal and target setting, 125–28; of government networks, 155; key areas, 124; Medicare and, 130–31; mitigation strategies, 142b; models, 123t; oversight costs, 128–29; in personnel systems, 175; in public sector, 121–22, 148; risk and risk sharing, 136–45; structuring incentives, 130–36; unintended consequences, 139–40; values and trust, 128–30. *See also* Management and governance
ACS. *See* Affiliated Computer Services
AEC. *See* Atomic Energy Commission
Affiliated Computer Services (ACS), 113
Afghanistan, 12
Africa, 13
Agencies, government: collaboration between, 98; core competencies, 184–85; employment issues, 171; in joined-up government, 15; leadership of, 159–62; management issues, 49–50, 164; network integration, 185; roles, 8; twisted incentives problem, 136b, 156; view of partnerships and contracts, 151. *See also* Bureaucracies; Government; Public sector

Alexander, Jennifer, 27
Al Qaeda, 8
AmeriCorps, 123, 161
Anthrax. *See* Terrorism
Arizona, 14, 72–73, 75, 85, 146
Armstrong, Neil, 32
Arquilla, John, 8–9
Atkeson, Edward B., 13
Atomic Energy Commission (AEC), 32
Australia, 15–16, 203n5
Automobile industry, 29, 40, 75

BAA (airport management company), 29, 86, 134–35
Baby boomers, 14–15
Baghdad. *See* Iraq
Beam, Steve, 78
Bedfordshire (U.K.), 107
Birmingham (U.K.), 19
Blair, Tony, 15
Blanchard, Angela, 85, 103
Bloomingdale, Mark, 102